10 95

Illuminations
of Hildegard of Bingen

Text by Hildegard of Bingen
with commentary by Matthew Fox, O.P.

BEAR & COMPANY, SANTA FE, NEW MEXICO

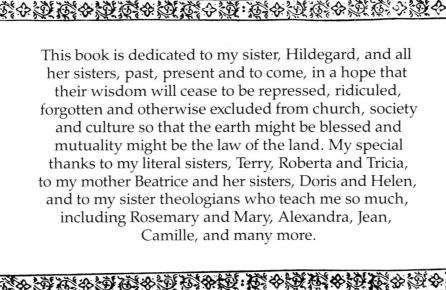

This book is dedicated to my sister, Hildegard, and all
her sisters, past, present and to come, in a hope that
their wisdom will cease to be repressed, ridiculed,
forgotten and otherwise excluded from church, society
and culture so that the earth might be blessed and
mutuality might be the law of the land. My special
thanks to my literal sisters, Terry, Roberta and Tricia,
to my mother Beatrice and her sisters, Doris and Helen,
and to my sister theologians who teach me so much,
including Rosemary and Mary, Alexandra, Jean,
Camille, and many more.

35mm transparencies of the illuminations
in this book are available by writing:
Friends of Creation Spirituality
PO Box 19216, Oakland, CA 94619.

Visions Five, Six, and Seven are reproduced by permission of
SCALA/Art Resources, New York City. All other visions are
reproduced by permission of Otto Muller Verlag, Salzburg;
all rights reserved by Otto Muller Verlag.
Library of Congress Number 85-156689
Copyright ©1985 by Bear & Company, Inc.
ISBN 0-939680-21-1

Bear & Company, Inc.
PO Drawer 2860
Santa Fe, NM 87504

Cover and interior design: William Field, Santa Fe
Typography: Copygraphics, Santa Fe
Printed in the United States of America
20 19 18 17 16 15 14 13 12 11 10

TABLE OF CONTENTS   PAGE

BOOKS BY THE SAME AUTHOR

Original Blessing: A Primer in Creation Spirituality
Meditations with Meister Eckhart
Breakthrough: Meister Eckhart's Creation Spirituality in New Translation
Manifesto For a Global Civilization (with physicist Brian Swimme)
A Spirituality Named Compassion and the Healing of the Global Village, Humpty Dumpty and Us
Western Spirituality: Historical Roots, Ecumenical Routes (editor)
Whee! We, wee all the Way Home: A Guide to Sensual, Prophetic Spirituality
On Becoming a Musical, Mystical Bear: Spirituality American Style
Religion USA: An Inquiry into Religion and Culture by Way of Time Magazine

I

HILDEGARD: HER TIMES AND HER ILLUMINATIONS

I. Hildegard: Her Times and Her Illuminations

ight hundred years ago, in the lush Rhineland valley, there lived a woman of extraordinary spirit and courage. In a century that gave birth to what has rightly been called the greatest Christian Renaissance, Hildegard of Bingen, whose lifetime spanned eighty percent of that century (1098-1179), stands out. In her lifetime, Chartres Cathedral rose from the grain fields of France with its delicious stained glass and its inimitable sculpture; Eleanor of Aquitaine and Thomas à Becket strode the political stage; Frederick Barbarossa frightened peasant and pope alike—and Hildegard dressed him down; Bernard of Clairvaux both reformed monastic life and launched the Second Crusade; the Cathedral School of Paris was evolving into the University of Paris—and its faculty approved of Hildegard's writings after she travelled there in her mid-seventies with her books under her arm;

Heloise and Abelard fell in love and left their tragic story for generations to ponder.

Through all the turmoil and all the creativity of the period, Hildegard carried on her work of preaching and teaching, of organizing and reforming, of establishing monasteries and journeying, of composing, writing, healing, studying, cajoling, and prophecying. Hildegard has left us over one hundred of her letters to emperors and popes, bishops, archbishops, nuns, and nobility. In addition, we have seventy-two songs including a morality play set to music that can rightly be called an opera and for which Hildegard has recently been acclaimed for "extending the vocabulary of medieval music radically beyond the norms" and for creating a "highly individual and unorthodox musical style."[1] She left us over seventy poems and nine books. Three of the latter are major theological works, *Scivias*, which we will discuss below; *Liber Vitae Meritorum* on ethics; and *De Operatione Dei*, also to be discussed below. Among her other books is one on physiology, *Liber Simplicis Medicinae*. This book, also called *Physica*, combines botanical and biological observations along with pharmaceutical advice. In it she treats at length of stones, trees, plants, and herbs. She also wrote a book on health called *Liber Compositae Medicinae* or *Causae et Curae* in which she discusses the symptoms, causes, and cures of physical ailments. She was the author of an interpretation of the *Rule of St. Benedict*, a commentary on the gospels, one on St. Athanasius' Creed, and two biographies of saints.[2]

A brief summary of her life would read as follows. She was born in the summer of 1098 at Bickelheim, on the left bank of the Nahe River, a tributary of the Rhine. The Nahe River flows into the Rhine at the town of Bingen. Her father was a German knight attached to the Castle of Bickelheim. Hildegard was the youngest of ten children and she admits to having had visionary experiences even as a little girl. Hildegard was educated under a tutor named Jutta, a holy anchoress with a cell consisting of several rooms attached to the Benedictine monastery of Mount St. Disibode. The Celtic connection is strong in Hildegard and her subsequent descendants of Rhineland mystics—Disibode was a Scotch-Irish monk who preached the Gospel in Hildegard's region in the seventh century and who presumably settled on what is still known to be Mount St. Disibode. Hildegard wrote songs to St. Disibode and she wrote his biography. She did the same for another Celtic monk, St. Rupert, after whom she named her own monastery. Rupert had journeyed all the way to Salzburg, Austria where he founded the monastery which was later to house the cathedral choir for whom Mozart composed much of his music. At the age of eight, Hildegard joined Jutta and another woman in her quarters in the monastery (Celtic monasteries had no qualms about housing men and women in one community, though under separate roofs) and there she was educated in the Benedictine traditions of music, spinning, Biblical history, prayer, and work. At about eighteen years of age, Hildegard took the Benedictine habit.

In 1136 Jutta died and Hildegard was appointed to take over leadership of the female community, now numbering about one dozen persons. Within four years Hildegard had her celebrated spiritual awakening (see Vision Two below) in which she took command of her vocation and creative life. From this time on she took responsibility to share the visions and thoughts that had been incubating in her for years. She started to write. A secretary was appointed her, a young monk named Volmar, who took down what she dictated and put it into correct Latin grammatical form. Her first book was born over a ten-year period. She worked industriously on it from her forty-second to her fifty-second year. She called it *Scivias* (Know the Ways), and in it are contained most of the illuminations reproduced in this book. In the midst of this creative period, Pope Eugenius III came to Trier on the way to launching the Council of Rheims. Hearing of the celebrated woman at Disibode, he sent a commission to investigate. This commission, on interviewing Hildegard, found her competent and authentic and so reported to the pope. Her works were brought to the pope and his retinue, including Bernard, Abbot of Clairvaux, and the pope's former teacher, and they were given papal approval. In his letter of approval, the pope encouraged Hildegard to keep writing. This she did. But she also wrote the pope admonishing him to work harder for reform in the church and its monasteries.

With Hildegard's fame spreading, her community of sisters rapidly increased in number and she did not want to stay in the women's cramped quarters of Mount St. Disibode where the male quarters had expanded to cover almost all the available land space. She had her eye on Mount St. Rupert near Bingen and the Nahe River where she was raised. The monks of Disibode and their Abbot Kuno fought her tooth and nail on her decision to leave their monastery. She flatly refused their pleadings and demands to stay, and she and her sisters left Disibode for Rupertsburg around 1151, taking their dowries with them. In her new establishment Hildegard was consecrated abbess and her activities took on the air of a very determined leader. She recognized only the Archbishop of Mainz as her superior and freed her community totally from the control of her former abbot. She also secured the protection of the Emperor for her community. The monastery itself, whose construction she oversaw, contained such new features as plumbing that piped in water. That she saw her defiance of the abbot as a struggle in justice is clear from a letter she wrote him. The opening paragraph uses the word "justice" five times. "I heard a voice speaking against the crimes which members of religious communities as well as lay people commit against justice: O justice, you are without a homeland; you are a foreigner in the city. . . 'Whence do I come? I come from the heart of the Father. And all lands are gathered around me. . . I sigh at the ignorance of the people.' " She ends her letter to the abbot and her former community with an admonition to "be converted to your God and be a light of the King"—earlier in her letter she declares that "justice is the purple-clad beloved of the King."[3] She criticized the monks for their return to practices that the Cluny reform had put an end to; the use, for example, of stewards and bailiffs to administer monastic lands.[4] The strife between these two communities was not settled until shortly before Hildegard's death, thirty-three years later.

In their new monastery, Hildegard's community flourished and her creativity took on new life and richer breadth. She now had a second secretary, a sister named Richarda. She founded still another monastery just across the river from Bingen at Eibingen in 1165 and endowed it sufficiently to maintain thirty sisters. She would cross the Rhine twice weekly to visit there. Her own monastery held about fifty sisters, women with considerable musical, singing, and painting gifts.

Bingen was an important river town because the Rhine River in Hildegard's day was impassible just below Bingen. Thus travelers portaged through Bingen on the way down the Rhine.

From her headquarters in Rupertsburg, Hildegard set out to preach to clergy, laity, monks, nuns and ecclesial officials all over the land. Usually she did her preaching in the cathedrals such as in Bamber; at Trier before the archbishop and a larger congregation at Wurzberg; at Ingleheim; and throughout Lorraine. In her talks she emphasized the corruption of the church, which she pictured as a weeping mother in pain, and the faithlessness of priests. She preached as far south as Constanz in Switzerland. She preached in Cologne where St. Ursula's basilica was held in great esteem; in Siegberg, Bonn, Anderbach, Metz, Bavaria, and in the Black Forest. Her preaching deeply affected the people who heard her and church leaders asked her for texts of her sermons. Benedictines and the new orders of Premonstratentions throughout these areas also invited her to preach in their monasteries. In her mid-seventies she journeyed to Tours and then to Paris. She had by now outlived her secretary, Volmar, and a Benedictine monk named Wibert had replaced him (sister Richarda, against Hildegard's wishes, had been named abbess of her own monastery some years before). There is evidence of friction between Hildegard and the highly educated Wibert who, unlike Volmar, took it upon himself to do more editing of Hildegard's works than she countenanced.

The year before she died, when she was in her eighties, Hildegard and her sisters of Rupertsburg were interdicted by the choirbishop of Mainz and then by Archbishop Christian who, even though he was her archbishop, was living in Italy. The controversy centered around Hildegard and her community's decision to bury in their cemetery a revolutionary youth who had been excommunicated by the archbishop. Hildegard refused to dig up the body and eject it from her convent grounds, insisting that he had confessed, been anointed, and communicated before dying. To prevent the choir chapter of Mainz from digging up the body themselves, she personally went to the cemetery and removed all traces of the burial. In her letter to the archbishop, Hildegard laments how, by the interdiction, he had silenced the most wonderful music on the Rhine; how all prophets wrote music and need music, but that music was now silenced on the Rhine. She concludes the letter with an admonition: Those who choose to silence music in this lifetime will go to a place where they will be "without the company of the angelic songs of praises in heaven." The interdict was removed and Hidegard died on September 17, 1179. Hildegard has never been formally canonized although three attempts were made to bring this about, one under Pope Gregory IX, another under Pope Innocent IV, and a third under Pope John XXII in 1317. Still, her cult was allowed and from the fifteenth century her name was included in the Martyrologies and in the Acta Sanctorum under the title of "Saint." In 1979 Pope John Paul II, in celebration of the 800th anniversary of Hildegard's death, referred to her as "an outstanding saint," a "light to her people and her time [who] shines out more brightly today."[5]

It is appropriate to remember Hildegard with light imagery since that is how she describes her spiritual awakening (see Vision Two below). "When I was forty-two years and seven months old, a burning light of tremendous brightness coming from heaven poured into my entire mind. Like a flame that does not burn but enkindles, it inflamed my entire heart and my entire breast, just like the sun that warms an object with its rays." What did this illumination do for Hildegard? "All of a sudden, I was able to taste of the understanding of the narration of books. I saw the psalter clearly and the evangelists and other catholic books of the Old and New Testaments." Hildegard was overcome by this experience of intuition, connection-making, and insight and went to bed sick. It was when she "placed my hand to writing" that she received new strength,[6] got out of bed, and spent the following ten years writing her first book called *Scivias*.

Why do we refer to her visions as "illuminations"? For Hildegard, it is the Holy Spirit who illumines.[7] Like the original Pentecost event, which Hildegard draws in her self portrait (see Vision Two below), she was awakened by the parted tongues of fire that make sense of Babel and allow deep communication to happen among the peoples. Frequently Hildegard pictures the Holy Spirit as fire: "O Holy Spirit, Fiery Comforter Spirit, Life of the life of all creatures," she writes. "Who is the Holy Spirit? The Holy Spirit is a Burning Spirit. It kindles the hearts

of humankind. Like tympanum and lyre it plays them, gathering volumes in the temple of the soul. . . .The Holy Spirit resurrects and awakens everything that is."[8] Surely all these statements about the fiery Holy Spirit apply to Hildegard's own experience with her visions and her call to speak and to inflame humankind with compassion. Hildegard celebrates God as "the living light and the obscured illumination" who has appointed her to speak to the peoples.[9] Her illuminations, then, are meant to rescue divinity from obscurity, to allow the divine to flow from human hearts—beginning with her own—once again. Like the light of the sun, she tells us, her heart was entirely inflamed and she felt the need to enkindle other hearts so that the imagination and creativity, forgiveness and contrition might flow again in the world. In her first vision she describes the spiritual awakening as an invitation to "come to light in the knowledge of mysteries. . .where with a bright light this serenity will shine forth strongly among those who shine forth."[10] Hildegard calls herself a female prophet ("prophetam istam") and her contemporaries agreed, comparing her to the prophet Deborah and to Jeremiah. She compares herself to Judith who slew Holophernes, the general of the Assyrian army, thus saving Israel. And she compares herself to David who slew Goliath.[11] She is deeply indebted to the apocalyptic prophets such as Daniel and Ezekiel for their vivid imagery as well. (Cf. Ez. 1.24-2.3, Dan. 8.15-27) Hildegard herself discouraged those who wanted to define her gifts as a foretelling of the future; instead, she understood her prophetic role as one of criticizing the present in such depth that the future might affect a deeper commitment to bringing about the Kingdom of God in the here and now.

Hildegard's teaching forced people to "wake up," take responsibility, make choices. Prophets "illuminate the darkness," she tells us. They are the people who can say, "God has illuminated me in both my eyes. By them I behold the splendor of light in the darkness. Through them I can choose the path I am to travel, whether I wish to be sighted or blind by recognizing what guide to call upon by day or by night." Here we learn the title of her book *Scivias*, which means "Know the Ways." Hildegard means "know the wise ways as distinct from the foolish ways." People who follow the ways of wisdom "will themselves become a fountain gushing from the waters of life...For these waters—that is, the believers —are a spring that can never be exhausted or run dry. No one will ever have too much of them...the waters through which we have been reborn to life have been sprinkled by the Holy Spirit."[12]

Hildegard's spiritual awakening is not without parallels in other cultures. Mircea Eliade, in examining the phenomena of cosmic illuminations among diverse groups including an Eskimo shaman, St. Paul, an American businessman, a Canadian psychiatrist, and Arjuna from the Bhagavad-Gita, draws some general conclusions. "It is important to stress that whatever the nature and intensity of an experience of the Light, it always evolves into a religious experience. All types of experience of the Light that we have quoted have this factor in common: they bring a man (sic) out of his worldly Universe or historical situation, and project him into a Universe different in quality, an entirely different world, transcendent and holy." The essence of the universe is now spiritual. The following result is fundamental to all these awakenings: "Whatever his previous ideological conditioning, a meeting with the Light produces a break in the subject's existence, revealing to him (sic)—or making clearer than before—the world of the Spirit, of holiness and of freedom; in brief, existence as a divine creation, or the world sanctified by the presence of God."[13]

Twenty-one of the illuminations or visions presented in this book and much of the text come from Hildegard's first book, *Scivias*, written while she was still living at Mount St. Disibode. The remaining visions—Five, Six, Seven, and the text accompanying them—are from her work *De Operatione Dei*, completed in 1170. Other commentaries from Hildegard that I have included in the text come from her letters, songs, and poems. Regarding the illuminations from *Scivias*, it has been established that all the visions were produced at the same time since the scribe doing the textual work left room on the page in each instance for the appropriate miniature. We do not know exactly who did the actual painting. It was most likely either the monks of the abbey of St. Eucharius in Trier, whose abbots were friends of Hildegard, or her own sisters at Rupertsburg. What is most important, however, is that Hildegard describes in great detail each of the images, and that she supervised the entire operation of the paintings.

"It is certain that their painting was directed by Hildegard herself," contemporary scholarship has established.[14] These illuminations have been called a "new Creation" because objects that characterized medieval iconography were re-formed by Hildegard and given a new presentation in her images. She gave birth to new symbolic forms and pictures which were unknown in the Middle Ages.[15]

The *Scivias* text we possess can be traced to the first half of the twelfth century. It is called the "R" or Rupertsburg codex. The text was preserved for centuries but in the Second World War it was taken to Dresden for safekeeping and has not been seen since. Fortunately, however, a photocopy had been made in 1927 in its original size and from 1927-1933 the Benedictine sisters of Eibingen produced a complete parchment reproduction of both the text and of the illuminations. It is now established once and for all that for the text we possess, a copy was completed in 1165 under Hildegard's direct supervision by the monk Wibert von Gembloux. The place for the writing of the text was the scriptorium of the monastery at Rupertsburg.[16] The original size of the manscript was very close to the size of the present book—12.8 inches by 9.25 inches. It was 235 parchment pages in length with double columns.

The text we possess for *De Operatione Dei* has been established scientifically as dating from 1170-1173. It was completed at Rupertsburg under the supervision of Hildegard herself. The illuminations from this book, three of which I reproduce here, do not date from Hildegard's time but were done in the year 1200 and are found in the Lucca Manuscript of *De Operatione Dei*, which is held at the Biblioteca Governativa in Lucca, Italy.[17] These pictures, which were drawn after Hildegard's death, contain her "signature" in the left-hand corner of each page because the artist wanted to emphasize how fully indebted he/she was to the detailed explanations Hildegard gave to the images. In other words, these pictures represent Hildegard's explicit naming of her visions.

The brief titles given each illumination are my own since Hildegard does not name them so succinctly. This titling of the images has a precedent, as the editor of the German edition of *Scivias*, Wisse die Wege, also named each vision. My titles are drawn from the theological context of Hildegard's commentary and are very often taken directly from her text.

II
HILDEGARD'S GIFTS FOR OUR TIMES

ildegard, mystic and a prophet, wishes to be a practical, helping mystic and prophet. She constantly extols the virtue of "usefulness" and in the final sentence of her major work, *De Operatione Dei*, she tells us that the reason for her work has been "for the usefulness of believers" who are asked to receive her words with a "modest heart."[18] She writes that God "destroys uselessness."[19]

Hildegard gives us a working guide to her work when she insists on usefulness. It is one thing to translate Hildegard or to be with her pictures and music—it is quite another to deeply understand her words and have them affect your psyche, religion, and culture to the extent that they are "useful," as she herself put it. Not everything a twelfth century nun speculated about is of equal value to our journeys and struggles today. But just how should we understand a mystic of eight centuries ago? How should we interpret her?

Even in her own time there were plenty of complaints from those who heard or read Hildegard but did not understand her message in the usefulness with which it was intended. Abbot Berthold of Zwiefalten wrote her that, "although I am often put in a joyful mood by the consolation of your words, I am sometimes depressed again because their obscurity closes them to my understanding."[20]

The recovery of the creation-centered spiritual tradition in our time is the greatest help in our understanding Hildegard of Bingen. She, being a Benedictine and a woman true to her experience, is a rich spokesperson of that tradition. Even though she lived in an era when Augustine dominated theology, Hildegard de-emphasizes fall/redemption religion in favor of creation-centered theology. Augustine, the great introspective genius, is silent on the cosmic Christ—but for Hildegard, the cosmic Christ forms the center of her thought. It is remarkable, for example, to compare her sense of cosmic justice and love of nature to her contemporary, Peter Lombard, whose works became for centuries the basic textbook of Christian clerics. As long as theology had only a fall/redemption approach to spirituality, it was not possible to understand Hildegard's immense contribution to spirituality. Now that we do, however, the serious student of Hildegard will find all four paths and every one of the twenty-six themes of the creation-centered spiritual tradition in her work. Like a magnet held up to her pages, these themes

draw out the most "useful" insights of her theology. These paths and themes, which I have delineated elsewhere in my book, *Original Blessing, A Primer in Creation Spirituality,*[21] include the following: Dabhar, the creative energy or word of God; blessing; earthiness as the meaning of humility; cosmos; trust; panentheism; royal personhood; realized eschatology; cosmic hospitality; emptying; being emptied; nothingness; divinization; art as meditation; trust of images; dialectic; God as Mother; New Creation; trusting the prophet call; anawim; compassion as celebration; compassion as erotic (Hildegard says "zealous") justice. Applying these themes to Hildegard's work makes her theology become alive, incarnated, fleshy, and "useful."

We need to understand how the creation-centered tradition offers a different agenda by which to understand some of the greatest minds in our Western heritage. It offers a hermeneutic or interpretation for seizing the essence of our creation-centered ancestors—an interpretation which is missing wherever creation spirituality is untaught. Without this "grid," interpreters of Hildegard miss her poignancy simply because they only know stale categories of fall/redemption theology. In researching and writing this book, I have personally been overwhelmed by the richness of Hildegard's deep theological development of every single one of the themes of the creation tradition. I have been profoundly moved by the amount of Eckhart in Hildegard, that is to say the themes that she pays attention to that later appear in Meister Eckhart's work. Indeed, Hildegard and Eckhart are sister and brother mystic/prophets. I heartily recommend reading this book a second time through with my volume of Meister Eckhart's sermons, *Breakthrough: Meister Eckhart's Creation Spirituality in New Translation*. I have learned from preparing this work on Hildegard that she has to be considered the pre-eminent woman theologian of the West up to the twentieth century. Her scope of intellectual, artistic, scientific, and political interest and involvement is astounding. I believe that someday soon she will follow in the footsteps of Catherine of Siena and Teresa of Avila in being named a Doctor of the Church.

Hildegard called herself a prophet, as did her contemporaries. It should be pointed out that in many respects prophets do not know what they are saying or what they are doing. By that I mean the prophet as prophet is touching something so deep in the human and cultural psyche that the full implications of what he/she unleashes do not make themselves evident in one's lifetime. Hildegard herself makes this very point, describing how the prophetic work is done "in the shadows" and how only later the human family makes clear the prophet's message and the divine wisdom elicited thereby.[22] Just as the truths in John of the Cross' poetry far exceed his rational commentaries on it, so too the depths of Hildegard's images and symbolism often outrace her commentaries on the illuminations. An example would be Vision Nine—how could Hildegard know the full impact of her term "fireball" for what comes into the human soul at birth? How could anyone know until twentieth century science established in the past decade how present the original fireball is to all life on our planet? The limits of Hildegard's conscious knowledge of what she was doing and of her culture's science puts great responsibility on those who choose to pray her illuminations and meditate on them today. She advises her readers to "lay hold of my warnings, embrace them, trace them in the enjoyment of your soul."[23] Reading this book needs to be an active process. That is why the reader needs to trust her or his experience with the illuminations, as well as to listen to the text. In my commentaries I invite the reader to enter the process of mysticism or unitive experience. I draw primarily on Hildegard's words, but I also employ authors who shed light on her theology and I encourage the reader to make this book as "useful" as possible.

In a letter written to her sisters, Hildegard talks about her death and she expresses her wish that "my voice may never fall into forgetfulness among you; may it rather be heard often in your midst in love."[24] Today our forgetfulness of Hildegard is coming to an end. Today there is a ferment of interest in Hildegard of Bingen. Records of her music are outselling pop stars; her opera is being performed on various continents; most of her books now exist in critical German and Latin editions and are being translated into English; her mystical writings are being studied, prayed, and danced to; plays are being written of her work and life; and, with this book, her illuminations are being made available to many. What accounts for

this amazing renaissance in Hildegard's life and spirituality? What is the powerful message that Hildegard stands for today?

Essentially, what Hildegard does is fill most of the gaps in Western religion. Gaps that have left the cosmos and cosmic Christ out of theology; gaps that have ignored humanity's divinity and creativity; gaps that have repressed humanity's relationship to all of creation; gaps that divorce salvation from active, useful, and effective healing of peoples and societies; gaps that ignore women's experiences and images and ways of theologizing; gaps that have obliterated the creation-centered spiritual tradition.

Let us take a closer look at some of the gifts Hildegard offers us in her work. I count at least eight gifts that Hildegard presents us with today that we are desperate to receive.

1 She is a woman in a patriarchal culture and a male-run church who strove to be heard, who struggled to offer her own wisdom and gifts borne of the experience and suffering of women of the past. In a letter to St. Bernard of Clairvaux she complains of the burden she carries as a woman in a patriarchal culture. "I am wretched and more than wretched in my existence as a woman," she complains.[25] Like any member of the "anawim" or oppressed peoples anywhere, she struggled for years with the "I can't" or "I shouldn't" or "Who am I to. . .'" feelings that she had been taught. She relates how often she was confined to a sickbed because she succumbed to this covering up of her talents and her voice and how her conversion—which was in fact a decision to write her visions for the larger community— brought about a physical energizing and got her, literally, out of bed. Mechtild of Magdeburg, a Beguine and lay woman who would follow one hundred years after Hildegard, was also advised that she was uneducated and theologically illiterate and ought to keep quiet about her spiritual insight. She tells us in her journal that, after much prayer and soul-searching, and after getting different advice from a few counselors, she concluded the following: "I am forced to write these words regarding which I would have gladly kept silent because I fear greatly the power of vainglory. But I have learned to fear more the judgment of God should I, God's small creature, keep silent."[26] I believe Hildegard would concur—that sins of

silence and omission are the greatest sins of oppressed persons everywhere.

Hildegard's psycho-physical struggle is archetypal and holds deep implications for the psychology and liberation of the oppressed. Self-expression, art for the people's sake: here lies the most radical kind of liberation. In music and poetry, writings and preaching, organizing prophetic resistance lies one's co-creative powers. Hildegard's extensive gifts of music and cosmic imagery are wonderful to behold precisely because the contribution of women in the arts and in religion has been so conveniently forgotten, repressed, or ridiculed in the centuries that have intervened since her time. She challenges women to be their full selves, to influence culture as well as home life, to express experience and not hold back. She is in this way a champion of a holistic culture, where women and men alike share their wisdom in mutuality.

Hildegard has been called "the first medieval woman to reflect and write at length on women" and her correspondence reveals a lifestyle of political and social activism that was "unheard of in a woman of her time."[27] Hildegard teaches that men and women are biologically different but equal as partners in God's creative work. She writes: "Man cannot be called man without woman. Neither can woman be called woman without man."[28] Far from being "defective males," as Aristotle taught and Aquinas would repeat, women were intended by nature in the unfolding of creation. Marriage is like a garden of love which God has planted but which man and woman must cultivate to protect from drought. In sexual love man and woman unite as one being, just as wind and air do. Tradition had taught that women are more lustful than men but Hildegard teaches the opposite. She develops a theory of the four temperaments and how each alters a woman's sexual typology as well. While Hildegard at times espouses the rhetoric of women's subordination to men and rejects the idea that women should be ordained priests, her activities reveal another side to her convictions about male/female relationships. As one scholar has put it: "She castigated a pope for his timidity and an emperor for moral blindness. She taught scholars and preached to clergy and laity as no woman before her had ever done. . . . She claimed that now woman rather than man—obviously Hildegard herself—was to do God's

work. It is difficult not to see in her visionary experience and activism, as well as her claim for the mission of woman in a male-dominated age, a gesture of protest, the reaction of an intelligent and energetic woman who chafed under the restraints imposed on women by the culture in which she lived."[29] She taught that now a woman would prophesy for the scandal of men and in her two most severe images of the demonic, as I point out below in Visions Eighteen and Twenty, patriarchy is itself pictured in league with the devil.

Hildegard suffered from the ambivalence that many oppressed persons do, including her own admission that she lacked the theological equipment to "analyze" her own work well.[30] Thus her theological arguments are probably not as conclusive as her heart and head actions in determining what she truly believed in. As one scholar puts it, "Hildegard's own fulminations against pope and emperor, her defiance of bishops, her ceaseless complaints about a society run and ruled by men, her charge that her age, because of the failing of men, placed a special responsibility on frail creatures like herself. . .seemed to reflect a profound disillusionment with a social order which gave women few rights and no power.[31]

Perhaps what is most exciting about rediscovering Hildegard is how amazingly intact her works are today. So many of her letters and books, her music and her images are ours to contemplate. This fact moves one to meditate silently on all the experience of women's wisdom that went unrecorded and unheard over the ages. Hildegard is a spokesperson for those silent millions. She hints at what has been missed in a one-sided, patriarchal culture, church, or psyche.

2 Hildegard brings together the holy trinity of art, science, and religion. She was so in love with nature, so taken by the revelation of the divine in creation, that she sought out the finest scientific minds of her day, made encyclopedias of their knowledge (before there were any encyclopedias), followed the scientific speculations on the shapes and elements of the universe, and wedded these to her own prayer, her own imagery, her own spirituality and art. Her scientific thought evolved, as I indicate in the commentary on Vision Four below, and she says, "All science comes from God." In her respect for

science—and indeed hunger for it—Hildegard would anticipate the lifework of Thomas Aquinas who, in the next century, would turn Christianity on its head by trying to prove that the "pagan" scientist Aristotle was compatible with Christian faith.

We too live in a time of great scientific excitement and discovery. Einstein's displacement of Newton's mechanistic universe has unleashed spiritual aspirations and imagery from poet and physicist alike. After centuries of a religionless cosmos and an introverted, cosmic-less religion, we long to experience a cosmos of mystery and spirit coming together again. Science and spirituality are coming together again to create a shared vision. Hildegard would approve. She would be leading the way in this magnificent venture which gives hope to the people and wisdom to our ways. Moreover, she has demonstrated what the missing link between science and spirituality is: art. Only a trust of our creativity and our imagery, expressed in the multiple ways of the creative human spirit, can make science's models or paradigms live in the souls of the people. She teaches that it is art—music, for example— that "wakes us from our sluggishness" and overcomes apathy, that makes cold hearts warm and dry consciences moist again. The proper context for spirituality and faith is the cosmos—not the privatized, individual soul. And the only way to express this cosmic experience is through art and creativity. Humans become the musical instruments of God. The divine Spirit makes music through us. Hildegard does not talk about these matters in abstract terms—she practices them by the scientific/artistic/theological methodology she employs in her work. Her first theological work, *Scivias*, includes pictures, a play, and music along with analytic reflections. "The works of humankind shall not disappear," she warns. "Those things that tend toward God shall shine forth in the heavens, while those that are demonic shall become notorious through their ill effects."[32]

Einstein warned that "science without religion is lame; religion without science is blind." Hildegard would surely concur. But she would add that science and religion without art are ineffective and violent; and art without science and religion is vapid.

3 Hildegard broadens and deepens our understanding and practice of psychology. For her, psychology is not the mere coping with ego problems but the relating of microcosm and macrocosm. She sees the human body and the human psyche as creation-in-miniature. We are in the cosmos and the cosmos is in us. "Now God has built the human form into the world structure, indeed even into the cosmos," she declares, "just as an artist would use a particular pattern in her work."[33] If this be so, then we are interdependent with all of creation and it is from this law of interdependence that truly wise living will be learned and practiced. This law of the universe Hildegard declares in the following manner: "God has arranged all things in the world in consideration of everything else."[34] Psychologist Carl Jung wrote that the proper psychology for twentieth-century men and women is medieval. Why? Because we of the twentieth century, who have unleashed the cosmic powers of the atom but lack a cosmic moral sense and a cosmic psychic understanding, need desperately a psychology of microcosm/macrocosm. The twentieth-century writer G.K. Chesterton once predicted that Thomas Aquinas may be remembered as the person who gave the twentieth century back a cosmos. While I respect Aquinas' cosmic vision, I believe it is Hildegard rather than Aquinas who will accomplish this essential task for us. For Hildegard is more steeped in women's wisdom than Aquinas. She gives us not just concepts but ways of healing psyche and cosmos. Art is the way; her mandalas as pictured in this book are ways; her drama, music, poetry, and her implicit invitation to make art our way of passing on a cosmic vision are all ways.

The value of a microcosmic/macrocosmic world view is underscored by Professor M.D. Chenu when he states that such a consciousness makes "nature and history interlock."[35] In other words, Hildegard holds the key to healing the dangerous dualism between nature and history, creation and salvation, mysticism and prophecy, that has dominated much of Western intellectual life for centuries. This healing will not take place in an exclusively rational mode. That is one reason why Aquinas' scholasticism has failed to return a cosmos to the West. Still, the healing of the individual is also at stake in recovering a microcosm/macrocosm psychology. For if Aquinas is correct that the individual's fulfillment can only occur in "a universe that is itself unified,"[36] then the key to that healing experience of oneness must be Hildegard's kind of psychic cosmology. This is one reason she resorts to the mandala so often to express compassion or healing. (See Vision One below.)

4 Hildegard offers a radical opportunity for global religious ecumenism because she is so true to her own mystical roots and her own creative process. Every time I have shared Hildegard's work, Native Americans have responded that they hear in her words the words of their ancestors. Once I was sharing her illuminations and her commentary and a man came up to me and said: "Last week I buried my grandmother who is Native American. All during your presentation I heard my grandmother every time you quoted Hildegard or showed one of her images." Yet Hildegard also speaks deeply to Eastern religions as well. This is not a complete surprise for as I noted in my work on Meister Eckhart, the Celts who settled so deeply into the Rhineland area were closely linked in their spirituality to the Hindu.[37] Readers and pray-ers of Hildegard's illuminations will see many examples of mandalas, those "maps of the cosmos," developed in the East as well as in the medieval West to "liberate the consciousness"[38] and return us to a primeval consciousness which is fundamentally one of unity. Clearly Hildegard's illuminations played that role with herself, a role of reintegration and holistic relating, which is her intention in sharing them with others, that they too may be healed. For Hildegard, her mandalas become a primary means by which the microcosm/macrocosm, the human and the universe, are brought together again. But this is the primary reason why Hindu and Buddhist religions employ the mandala as well. As Giuseppe Tucci puts it in his classic work, *The Theory and Practice of the Mandala*, "the whole drama of the universe is repeated in ourselves."[39] This is the drama Hildegard felt deeply and for her it is the primary focus of her mandalas and drawings: the drama of creation unfolding in the human. "I have exalted humankind," she cites the Creator as saying, "with the vocation of creation. Humankind alone is called to co-create." And she warns humanity: "All nature is at the disposal of humankind. We are to work with it. Without it we cannot survive."[40]

C areful readers of Hildegard and viewers of her illuminations will see deep influences of the ancient goddess religions, of the Roman Aurora, the Egyptian Isis, the old Germanic Horsel, and the Hebrew hokma or female Wisdom figure as well as Aztec and Native American symbols.

I t is of tremendous importance in our day to recover the wisdom of so ecumenical a figure as Hildegard of Bingen. Why? Because there can be no global peace and justice without global spirituality. And there will be no global spirituality without a new and deeper level of ecumenism occurring at that level of mysticism. The key ingredient that has up to now been sadly lacking in ecumenical exchange, except in rare instances such as the person of Thomas Merton, is mysticism. It has been missing in religious rapport because the West is so out of touch with its own deepest and most holistic mystics. It has so readily forgotten and dismissed its holistic, feminist tradition— the very tradition that Hildegard summarizes in her person and work— in effect launching the Rhineland mystical movement. Ecumenism need not mean dashing off to foreign shores to find spiritual nourishment —at least it need no longer mean that. With giants like Hildegard and Eckhart, Francis and Aquinas, Mechtild and Dante, Julian and Nicolas of Cusa, the West can cease its mystical embarrassment vis-à-vis the East. Hildegard challenges Westerners to take another and deeper look at their own spiritual roots, especially those nearly forgotten roots of the creation-centered spiritual tradition. Jung celebrates this re-examination or our own roots when he writes: "Of what use to us is the wisdom of the Upanishad or the insight of Chinese yoga, if we desert the foundations of our own culture as though they were errors outlived and, like homeless pirates, settle with thievish intent on foreign shores?"[41] Hildegard, as universal as she is, is also thoroughly grounded in the Western spiritual tradition. To ground ourselves in that tradition is the best and most certain way to be ecumenical in the fullest sense.

T he ecumenism Hildegard champions is not a religious affair to be worked out by the professionally ordained or religious ones. As we saw in the previous contributions Hildegard makes, her world is as scientific and artistic as it is religious. She helps us to broaden our understanding of ecumenism, bringing together all the creativity of the human being in touch with the cosmos. Perhaps what she accomplishes is best summarized in the Eastern sacred literature, in the Upanishad . "In the space that is within the heart lies the Lord of All, the Ruler of the Universe, the King of the Universe. . . .Truly like the extent of space is the void within the heart. Heaven and earth are in it. Agni and Vayu, the sun and the moon, likewise also the stars and the lightning and all other things which exist in the universe and all that which does not exist, all exists in that void."[42] Tucci comments on what has been described here: "In the space of the heart, magically transfigured into cosmic space, there takes place the rediscovery of our interior reality, of that immaculate principle which is out of our reach, but from which is derived—in its illusory and transcendent appearance—all that is in process of becoming."[43] I have never shared Hildegard's illuminations, thoughts, sayings, or music with anyone whose interior space was not touched. Why is this? Because Hildegard was first and foremost a mystic who trusted her experience and images. She invites us to do the same. Her power cuts through time and space as conventionally understood. Often when I have shown her illuminations, people have responded this way: "I had a dream a few nights ago with one of these images in it and I did not know what it meant or where it came from. But now I know it has been Hildegard speaking to me in advance of tonight's experience." Precognition is part of the energy that the communion of saints wants to share with us today. Heaven knows we can use all the help we can get!

5 Hildegard is not only mystic; she is also prophet and she sees herself and her work consciously and deliberately as prophetic. She disturbs the complacent, deliberately provoking the privileged, be they emperors or popes, abbots or archbishops, monks or princes to greater justice and deeper sensitivity to the oppressed. She often compares her kind of prophecy to the apocalyptic prophet Ezekiel, whose highly symbolic denunciations attacked the corruption of religion in his time as Hildegard did in hers. Many persons have seen in Hildegard's denunciations a prerunner of the Reformation in Germany. It is true that at least one friend of Martin Luther, the Nurnberg preacher, Andreas Osiander, did invoke Hildegard as a precursor of the Protestant Reformation. A good argument could be made that one reason she has been so little heard during the past few centuries is that her brand of Christianity was too "protestant" for Catholics to trust. Now, however, that the ecumenical movement among Christians has reinforced the prophetic charism for Catholics and the mystical charism for alert Protestants, Hildegard's

contribution as prophet is all the more timely.

Hildegard was not a lone prophet. She inspired dozens and dozens of Benedictine sisters, monks, lay persons all around her to launch out and renew Christianity. Furthermore, she launched a political-mystical movement in the Rhineland that was in no way silenced after her death. As I have written elsewhere, she can rightly be called the "Grandmother of the Rhineland mystic movement," a movement that included Francis of Assisi, Mechtild of Magdeburg, Meister Eckhart, Julian of Norwich (indirectly), Nicolas of Cusa—all of whom brought the powers of mysticism to bear not on supporting the status quo but on energizing the prophetic in society and church. For Hildegard, justice plays a dominant role in her cosmos, her psychology, her theology of work and morality. Reading Hildegard, one can understand more fully Meister Eckhart's statement that "the person who understands what I say about justice understands everything I have to say." While the themes of justice and cosmic balance and harmony permeate all of Hildegard's work, perhaps it is best summarized in the last vision, Vision Twenty-Five below, where she celebrates the communion of saints as "the blessed ones, happy ones, who moved God in their time on earth and stirred God with sincere striving for just works."[44] Justice is the primary struggle of creation—to allow injustice to reign is to invite chaos to take over. (See Visions Four, Six, and Eighteen below.)

To celebrate Hildegard as prophet is not to say she was prophetic all of the time or right all the time. No human can claim such honors. One wishes, on reading her works, that she had been more resistant to the call for a second and deeply violent Crusade; that she had been more sensitive to anti-semitism in her language; that she had been more conscious of the systematic and structural causes of the oppression and decadence that she so heartily decried; and she had succumbed less to the prevailing rhetoric against women. Throughout her life, however, Hildegard remained true to her prophetic vocation. She never forsook her sisters in their constant struggle for psychic, political, and spiritual survival in a male-dominated church and society. Her songs celebrating Mary and Ursula far outnumber her songs to male divinity. Her letters to women are longer, more personal, more human than her instructions to men. She never lost faith with the anawim, nor they with her, as is evidenced in that last incident of her life when her defense of a revolutionary youth brought upon her the price of interdiction. She remained a sign of contradiction and of conscience in an all-male system and persevered to the end. She herself described what the prophet was and in doing so described her own life. "Who are the prophets? They are a royal people, who penetrate mystery and see with the spirit's eyes. In illuminating darkness they speak out."[45] Hildegard spoke out. Out of the darkness and pain of her own journey, she spoke out. And she sang out, and wrote out. And traveled out. And preached out. And resisted out to the end. She challenges us to be prophet in our way to our culture and our religions.

6 Hildegard is deeply *ecological* in her spirituality. The basic thrust of our time is the movement from an egological to an ecological consciousness. International author Laurens van der Post believes that ecological injustice reigns because we lack an ecological spirituality. "The reason we exploit, damage and savage the Earth is because we are out of balance. We have lost our sense of proportion. And we cannot be proportionate unless we honor the wilderness and the natural persons within ourselves." He also believes that the psychic price we pay for being out of touch with nature is a "staggering loss of identity and meaning. . .a kind of loneliness, an inadequate comprehension of what life can be."[46] It is clear that humanity needs all the help it can get from the past, from the communion of saints, to usher us from our preoccupations with the human, from our awesome anthropocentrism, to a more cosmic and creation-centered way of existence. No one is better equipped to be our guide than Hildegard of Bingen. For no one was more in tune with the symphony of the universe than she. No period in human history in the West was more awakened to the divine in nature than Hildegard's century. The great scholar of the twelfth century, Fr. M.D. Chenu, characterizes that period's nature awakening in the following ways: "The simplest but not the least significant evidence of this discovery of nature was their perception of the universe as an entity."[47] Is this not what characterizes the amazing discoveries of our time, that the vast, vast universe is one being, one entity? Chenu goes on: "The whole penetrates each of its parts; it is one universe; God

conceived it as a unique living being. . . .Because it is a single whole, the harmony of this universe is striking."[48] Is this not what the ecological consciousness is about today? About seeing the world as it is, as interdependent and interconnected? What was being discovered and celebrated in Hildegard's time and is so deeply needed in ours is what Chenu calls "the sacramental character of the universe." This is not a matter of human projection onto the universe but it is an issue of the intrinsic holiness of matter and harmony itself. "For, even before people contemplate it, the sacramental universe is filled with God."[49]

Hildegard is rich in expressing the intrinsic holiness of being. For example, she writes: "I, the fiery life of divine wisdom, I ignite the beauty of the plains, I sparkle the waters, I burn in the sun, and the moon, and the stars." And again, "There is no creation that does not have a radiance. Be it greenness or seed, blossom or beauty, it could not be creation without it." And again, "the word is living, being, spirit, all verdant greening, all creativity. All creation awakened, called, by the resounding melody God's invocation of the word."[50]

Hildegard celebrates the inherent divinity and beauty of all creation, and she does so in the context of an erotic philosophy. For she says that God and creation are related as lover to lover. Yet, she also maintains an historical approach. She does this because her prophetic sense is never compromised in her appreciation of what is. Chenu puts it this way. "The extravagant visionary temperament of Hildegard of Bingen transformed the learned physical science she used as the stuff of her symbolism and made it express rather the developing history of Christianity than the static universe of the Greeks."[51] Hildegard has a deep historical sense and she insists on making clear the moral responsibility of the human race. She shouts, "The earth must not be injured, the earth must not be destroyed!" She warns humanity that its sins of indifference and injustice to nature will cause hardships on humanity itself, for creation demands justice.[52] While the evolutionary and historical sense lies even deeper in the psyche of modern persons than with Hildegard, still it is good news to know that she, thanks to her prophetic grounding, does not dismiss the historical or use mysticism as a flight from time or social responsibility.

Clearly, if one is looking for a spiritual guide or a patron saint of the needed ecological awakening of our time, we could do no better in searching the pantheon of Western Christianity than to nominate Hildegard of Bingen.

7 Hildegard challenges our theological methodology in particular and our entire educational methodology in general. Hildegard finds it impossible to theologize with intellect alone or one might say with left brain alone. As I indicated above, she breaks into imagery, mandala drawing, poetry, music, and drama in her very first theological work and never ceases this kind of learning and teaching the rest of her busy life. In doing education this way, by pictures and story as well as analysis, Hildegard is being true to her bonding with the anawim. Art as meditation is a political issue. For there are deep political implications in the way we choose to educate and Hildegard is speaking to the ordinary, often uneducated, people by the very means she chooses to teach with. Iconography was a popular art in the early part of the Christian era,[53] before Christianity and empire were so conveniently married. Hildegard returns to this tradition. Pictures and stories precede words as the manner in which individuals learn. Humanity "drew pictures long before [it] could write books, or carve inscriptions."[54] Hildegard is demonstrating to us *how* to make ecumenism happen—we must break out of our exclusively left-brain theologies and educational modes to make hearts and imaginations and heads dance with shared insight and illuminations. These are the ways that children first learn. One might call her methodology, a "folk education"—it excludes no one, not the old, the young, the uneducated, the peasant, not even the educated—unless the latter become all dried up after too many years of one-sided education.

In being true to art as a means of education, Hildegard is telling us something of women's wisdom. Education must include process as well as concept. Putting the two together is what moves people and *educes from them* (the true meaning of the word "education") what is their rich contribution to culture. By her holistic education practice, Hildegard invites the reader into a process. Even after 800 years, the process of her illuminations begs us to enter into our own awakening, our own illumina-tion. Such education personalizes and makes erotic the learning that we undergo. Hildegard sees our lives as a journey and an adventure (see Vision Nine below)—it is theology's task to articulate and to challenge the journey—not to stifle it or smother it with epistemological exercises or speculative abstractions.

I truly believe that her theological methodology renders obsolete ninety-nine percent of all that we are calling theological learning in the twentieth century. Why? Because experience and art and cosmos are at the core of her spirituality and not an ugly, sin-oriented, anthropocentrism. Though the science of her day was greatly limited, she made the most of it. Who could imagine the renaissance that could occur in our time if education once again became as rounded, balanced, holistic, and imaginative as it was for Hildegard?

8 Hildegard awakens us to symbolic consciousness. Preparing these illuminations and Hildegard's commentary on them has proven to be a veritable graduate course in symbolism for me. An awakening to symbolism is an awakening to deeper connection-making, to deeper ecumenism, to deeper healing, to deeper art, to deeper mysticism, to deeper social justice. Reading this book will be Hildegard's way of inviting our generation into a deeper process of symbolizing. Mircea Eliade would consider this a major contribution on Hildegard's part, for according to him, it is symbolic awakening that will put Western culture in touch with non-European peoples once again. It is the proper road to ecumenism and to spirituality itself. "The symbol, the myth and the image are of the very substance of the spiritual life... they may become disguised, mutilated or degraded, but never are extirpated."[55] What is gained by the reader who allows himself or herself to be led into Hildegard's rich world of symbolism? Eliade believes that the person "who understands a symbol not only 'opens himself' to the objective world, but at the same time succeeds in emerging from his personal situation and reaching a comprehension of the universal."[56] Paradox and personal experience, systematic imagination and diverse levels of meaning, cosmos and world patterns, are all expressed by symbol. Entering into Hildegard's symbolism awakens the rich symbolic treasury of Christian

history. Her century was peculiarly "saturated" with a symbolic consciousness, as Professor Chenu points out. "At stake is the discernment of the profound truth that lies hidden within the dense substance of things and is revealed by these means." We cannot understand Hildegard without understanding this "symbolist mentality" of her times. "The same people read the Grail story and the homilies of St. Bernard, carved the capitals of Chartres and composed the bestiaries, allegorized Ovid and scrutinized the typological senses of the Bible, or enriched their Christological analyses of the sacraments with naturalistic symbols of water, light, eating, marriage." What was at stake in all symbolizing was "the mysterious kinship between the physical world and the realm of the sacred." And Chenu asks this probing question: "How can one write the history of Christian doctrines, let alone that of theological science, without taking into consideration this recourse to symbols. . .which continually nourished both doctrine and theology?" Hildegard's invitation to a symbolic awakening is part of her prophetic contribution to our education, our theology, our living. She lives out in her life the solid criteria of the deep, sensual, prophetic spiritual journey that I have outlined elsewhere as: 1) Whee!—trusting one's experience of breakthrough, intuition, ecstasy, and union; 2) We—deepening one's symbolic consciousness; and 3) we—responding to one's prophetic call to critique the powers-that-be in one's culture.[58]

I have named eight gifts of pressing value that Hildegard bequeathes to our times: her experience as a woman and her personal struggle for liberation; her marrying of science, art, and religion; her psychology of microcosm/macrocosm; her potential for global religious ecumenism based on her deep mysticism; her prophetic commitment to justice; her deep ecological sense; her commitment to holistic education and theological methodology; her symbolic consciousness. For all these reasons, Hildegard gifts us today because she *heals*. She awakens and she heals. She awakens Christianity to some of the wisdom of the ancient women's religions and thereby offers healing to the male/female split in religion. She awakens the psyche to the cosmos and thereby offers healing to both. She awakens to the holiness of the earth and thereby heals the awful split between matter and spirit in the West. She awakens art to science and science to music and religion to science. And thereby heals the dangerous rift between science and religion that has dominated culture the past 300 years in the West. She heals the isolation of the artist from the deepest intellectual and spiritual currents of the past. She illumines. "In illuminating darkness, she speaks out." She illumines us today more than she illumined or dreamed of illuminating anyone in her own time. She gifts us with her illuminations.

Has there ever been a time in human history or the history of the planet when illumination, light, wisdom, was needed more than now? Can anyone be better equipped to lead us than the neglected one, St. Hildegard, who in fact defines the ultimate act of illumination as compassion (see Vision One)?

My role in this book has been to explain, to motivate, to encourage the readers into the directions of interaction with this great mystic in order to unleash their own mysticism. In my commentaries much is left unsaid and uncommented on—readers are urged to do their own connection-making and thus become participants with Hildegard in carrying on these living mandalas. Process and participation are Hildegard's way of encouraging us in our spiritual journeys. My method in this book has been to get out of the way as much as possible and to allow Hildegard to speak by her visions and her words. I have used primary sources for Hildegard's words entirely in this book. To assist the reader an index of basic themes and symbols is at the end of the text.

Hopefully this modest book will inspire deeper and deeper forays into the wonderful storehouses and treasures of the human race's mystical possibilities. And from contact with such riches we as a race might gather the splendor and trust, the beauty and imagination, to create a world worthy of ourselves and our planet and the divine splendor we carry in us and breathe in all around us. This would correspond to Hildegard's deepest desires, for it was she who said: "Divinity is aimed at humanity."

January, 1985
Institute in Culture and Creation Spirituality
Holy Names College, Oakland, CA

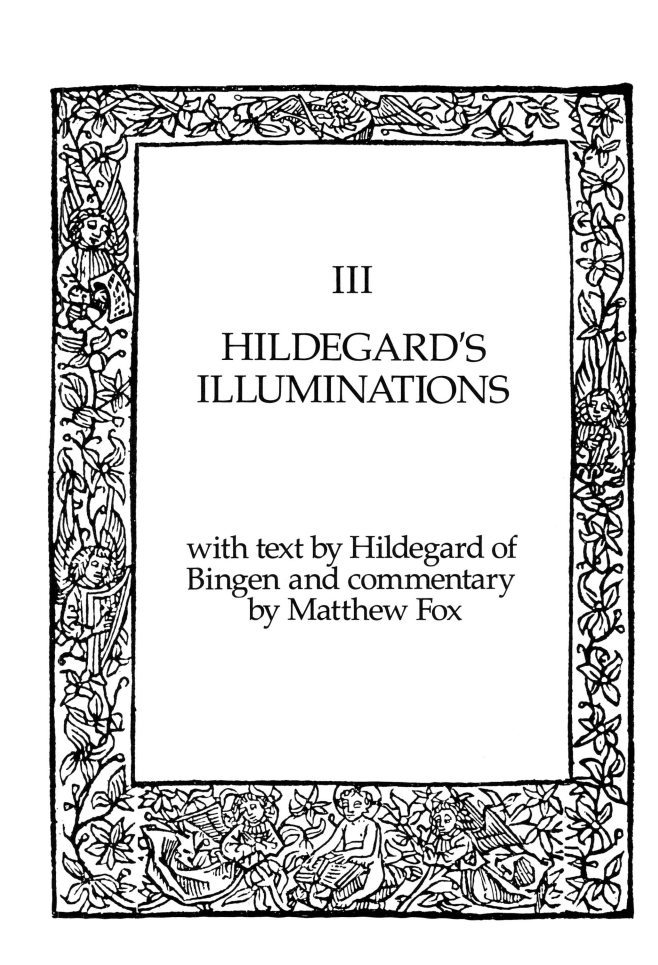

III

HILDEGARD'S ILLUMINATIONS

with text by Hildegard of Bingen and commentary by Matthew Fox

1. The Man in Sapphire Blue: A Study in Compassion

ildegard describes this illumination in the following manner: "A most quiet light and in it burning with flashing fire the form of a man in sapphire blue."[1] We experience in this mandala much that is peacemaking and powerful. The blue colors denote compassion as do the hands of the blue man, extended in a manner of healing and assisting. Notice that they are not presented in a vertical and folded manner of stylized piety, but in an extended way. An energy field surrounds the man. Clearly this is a person whose "body is in the soul" and not whose soul is in the body—both Hildegard and later, Meister Eckhart, spoke of the body/soul relationship in this imagery of shared energy systems, with the soul energy being the greater entity. Notice too the aperture at the man's head, so that this powerful healing energy can leave his own field and mix with others—and vice versa. A Native American commenting on this vision remarked that it reminded him of the sacred circle where there is only one entrance and one exit. The woven tapestry-like detail of the inner golden circle reminded him of basket weaving and the rituals of southwestern Indians. In such practices the cosmic web is being celebrated and renewed.

In another place Hildegard pictures the Trinity in this way: "The Father is brightness and this brightness has a flashing forth and in this flashing forth is fire and these three are one." In this vision she calls the Creator a "living" light; the Son, "flash of light"; the Spirit, "fire." She says that this fire of the Holy Spirit binds all things together—"The Holy Spirit streams through and ties together 'eternity' and 'equality' so that they are one. This is like someone tying a bundle together—for there would be no bundle if it weren't tied together—everything would fall apart."[2] The gold and silver circles do indeed resemble rope in this image. There is a long tradition in East Indian cosmology of cord and thread imagery, as Mircea Eliade has pointed out. "Their role is to implement *all living unity*, both cosmic and human. These primordial images serve at once to reveal the structure of the Universe and to describe the specific situation of man. Images of the rope and thread succeed in suggesting...that all things existing are, by their nature, produced, 'projected,' or 'woven' by a superior principle, and that all existence in Time implies an 'articulation' or 'web.' "[3] Hildegard herself refers to the "web of the universe" on more than one occasion. Thus her golden rope tells us of the interconnectivity of all being and of divinity with creation and humanity. In the same letter in which she talks about the Trinity of light, flashing, and fire and the binding principle in the fire of the Spirit, Hildegard also identifies wisdom with compassion. For to be foolish (the opposite of wise) is to "lack motherly compassion. Whoever lacks this dies of thirst."[4] This may be one reason she has chosen blue, a color for water, as a dominant color in this image of the compassionate cosmos.

Hildegard understands this mandala to represent the Divine Trinity. "One light, three persons, one God," she declares. It is important to Hildegard that God be imaged essentially as curved and circular. This is an ancient tradition wherever women's religions are allowed their say: the Divinity as circle, or circle in motion, that is, spiral. Hildegard writes elsewhere: "A wheel was shown to me, wonderful to behold. . . . Divinity is in its omniscience and omnipotence like a wheel, a circle, a whole, that can neither be understood, nor divided, nor begun nor ended."[5] And again, "just as a circle embraces all that is within it, so does the Godhead embrace all." The imagery of God as circle, God that embraces all, that encompasses all, is deeply maternal. "Godhead," which is feminine in both Latin and German, is an all-embracing name for divinity. We celebrate here the curved and all-encompassing power of God. Yet we also celebrate God's nearness, for Hildegard also says: "God hugs you. You are encircled by the arms of the mystery of God."[6] Thus God's power is not an abstract power or a vengeful power but a maternal, loving, and deeply personal power. It is a *compassionate* power. This power cannot in the long run be excluded from our lives or from our universe. For "no one has the power to divide this circle, to surpass it, or to limit it."[7]

Wisdom and compassion go together for Hildegard. She advises the archbishop of Salzburg on one occasion to let his work "be saturated at the fountain of wisdom. . . for wisdom, like love, has ordered all things and she has allowed countless little brooks to arise from her waters. For it is personified Wisdom which says, 'Alone have I made the circuit of the vault of heaven.' " But when are we wise and loving? "When you compassionately touch and cleanse the wounds of others, then I [love] am reclining on your bed. And when you meet simple, honest people with good will and in a godly way, then I am united to you in loving friendship." She goes on to explain how cosmic compassion and human compassion are to come together. "I, wisdom, bind together heavenly and earthly things as a unity for the good of the people. And so you should handle and cleanse the wounds of those who are sick; and you should maintain the innocent and righteous. And with God's help let your heart rejoice with the one as much as the other."[8] Thus for Hildegard, compassion is active—it binds the universe and the ailing human body. It cleanses, supports, celebrates. She also counseled the emperor Frederick Barbarossa in one of her letters to him to "imitate the highest Judge and Ruler in his compassion."[9]

For Hildegard and for the entire creation-centered tradition, the ultimate power of God, universe, and humanity is *compassion*. Meister Eckhart, following Hildegard's theology exactly on this point, would write 140 years later: "You may call God love; you may call God goodness; but the best name for God is Compassion."[10] Hildegard is not celebrating this divine power of compassion apart from ourselves—for her, "Divinity is aimed at humanity" and all of us are capable of divine compassion. She writes of how compassion affects a person: "I am flooded through with inner compassion; nothing—neither gold nor money, costly stones nor pearls—can hide from me the eyes of the poor who weep because they lack life's necessities."[11] Here Hildegard is being very practical about what interferes with compassion—it is our complacency and comfort that cuts us off from the pain of others, involvement with others, even celebration with others. Compassion for Hildegard involves our relationships with all creatures, it constitutes the way we see the world. Do we see it interconnected—the way it is? Or do we see it dualistically as possession-consciousness, "I *have*" instead of "I *am related to*. . .?" Hildegard celebrates our compassionate existence of trust and reverence with all creatures when she writes: "As human persons view creation with compassion in trust, they see the Lord. It is God which humankind is then able to recognize in every living thing."[12] Thus, all creation is a theophany for Hildegard, a source of divine revelation—but we know this only to the extent that we look on creation with a "compassionate trust."

Hildegard's theology of the Trinity, so energetically set forth in this mandala, is about the entrance of divine compassion into the world. Her Christology presented in this picture of the "blue Christ" is rich and clear. Jesus the Christ is the revelation of the compassion of God, the incarnation of divine compassion, the human person in whom divine compassion shines forth in a special way. It is through him that "the maternal love of the embracing God came" to humankind. Hildegard's identifying compassion with maternal love is a rich tradition when one remembers that the Hebrew word for compassion is the same root word as the word for "*womb*".[13] All the Trinitarian energies in this picture find their culmination in the healing and extended hands of the man in sapphire blue which form the mandala's center.

But Hildegard, by presenting her Trinity in a mandala form, is revealing still more about God to us. She is revealing how we too are divine and how we too are "other Christs." How is she able to do this? Because of what a mandala is and does. And because she consciously chose to present the Trinity in mandala form. Professor Tucci, an expert on the mandala in Eastern practice, writes that we do not merely look at a mandala—we are transformed by it. The mandala, he writes, "is a geometric projection of the world reduced to an essential pattern." For Hildegard, drawing her mandala out of the Biblical and prophetic tradition, the essential pattern of the world is the energy of divine compassion. To connect with this "essential pattern" is to find God again, to find salvation or healing for self and others. Tucci goes on: "When the mystic identified himself with its center, it transformed him and so determined the first conditions for the success of his work." Thus, Hildegard is telling us to make compassion the first condition for our work. And in doing this we make "the blue man," the Christ, the core energy source not only for ourselves but for the universe. There lies our transformation into sons or daughters of God. Tucci continues: "The person who used it [the mandala] no longer wanted to only return to the center of the universe. Dissatisfied with the experience of the psyche he longed for a state of concentration in order to find once more the unity of a secluded and undiverted consciousness, and to restore in himself the ideal principle of things. So the mandala is no longer a cosmogram but a psychocosmogram, the scheme of disintegration from the One to the many and reintegration from the many to the One, to that Absolute Consciousness, entire and luminous, which Yoga causes to shine once more in the depths of our being."[14] Hildegard is inviting us to let the depths of our being shine with the true person of Christ: Compassion. And the personal unity she invites us to seek is not a withdrawn act of meditation but an enjoinment in "the ideal principle of things," Compassion Personified. For Hildegard, it is Jesus Christ, healer. What illumination means is a shining compassion. "The compassion of the grace of God will make humans light up like the sun," she declares.[15]

Tucci explains more fully what Hildegard is accomplishing prayerfully and openly in herself and in us by this mandala. The person interacting with an icon or mandala, he writes, "places in the center of himself the recondite principle of life, the divine seed, the mysterious essence. He has the vague intuition of a light that burns within him and which spreads out and is diffused. In this light his whole personality is concentrated and it develops around that light."[16] Hildegard in this vision has blown up, so to speak, what the divine seed truly looks like, that recondite principle of life that constitutes the mysterious essence of divinity: it is compassion. Meister Eckhart, following on St. Peter's epistle, would celebrate how divine seed dwells within us and how it meant to develop into God. Hildegard names that seed: compassion. We are, therefore, not to gaze at this mandala; we are to become it, to carry it with us, to let it carry us with it, into ever-expanding spirals of active compassion. For there is, in Hildegard's words, only "one light, one God." But we are the divine hands, the divine sons or daughters, the ones destined to carry out divine compassion. Meister Eckhart writes: "Whatever God does, the first outburst is always compassion."[17] Thus our origins are most truly compassion; and our destiny; and our unity and wholeness, our healing and salvation. Compassion floods the universe. Hildegard invites us to let it flood (is that why blue is so prominent in and outside of the mandala?) our selves so that there is again only one primal energy, that of healing, celebrative, and flashing fire, called compassion.

By drawing the Trinity as a mandala Hildegard is instructing us that Divinity is not "out there" and Christ is not "out there" and the compassion and divine light the world desperately yearns for is not "out there." It is as near as is our capacity for centering on the essence of God and universe: compassion.

2. Hildegard's Awakening: A Self Portrait

In this picture Hildegard celebrates her conversion experience. As I pointed out in Part II, the moment of Hildegard's breakthrough is important not only to Hildegard but to all oppressed peoples. For it was art—that is, self-expression—that was the ultimate form of healing for Hildegard. She describes her condition of passivity, being without voice, frustrated, physically sick. In the name of humility she had made herself sick. "Not in stubbornness but in humility, I refused to write for so long that I felt pressed down under the whip of God into a bed of sickness." She tells us that even though she had experienced wonderful things, "because of doubt and erroneous thinking and because of controversial advice from men," she had refused to write. It was this letting go of masochism, the "I can't" syndrome, that marked her spiritual awakening, and ended her physical sufferings at that time. "Beaten down by many kinds of illnesses, I put my hand to writing. Once I did this, a deep and profound exposition of books came over me. I received the strength to rise up from my sick bed, and under that power I continued to carry out the work to the end, using all of ten years to do it."[1] Notice how the issue for an oppressed person is "strength and power"—how did Hildegard finally achieve both? By putting her hand to writing. By self-expression, by art as meditation. Notice that her strength returned while writing her book, that is

"in the process of" self-expression—it was not the product, a book completed ten years later that healed her—it was the "process" of art as meditation. The lessons here for all who feel "doubt," for all who are "beaten down," are hundredfold.

This picture, like the previous one that wove the divine essence of the Trinity into our own essence of compassion, makes the Holy Spirit Hildegard's and ours at the same time. For Hildegard does not hesitate to appropriate the Pentecost experience, the Spirit's fire that illumines and thaws and connects, to herself. It was when she was "inflamed by a fiery light" that she put her hand to writing. The parted tongues of fire are clearly a reference to the first Christian disciples' experience of Pentecost. But they are not in this picture; Hildegard is. Once again we see how doctrine for Hildegard is not primarily an object to be studied but the naming of an experience undergone. And, like the first recipients of this Spirit in the Book of Acts, the power of the spirit's awakening is not meant for oneself but for others. The first disciples, like Hildegard, were cured of their doubt and fear so as to preach Good News to "Parthians, Medes and Elamites; people from Mesopotamia, Judaea and Cappadocia, Pontus and Asia, Phrygia and Pamphylia, Egypt and the parts of Libya round Cyrene; as well as visitors from Rome—Jews and proselytes alike—Cretans and Arabs." (Acts 2.9-11)

And so Hildegard too begins her missionary activity, her being sent to the church to speak of its own inner beauty and corruption.

In picturing herself as a recipient of the Pentecostal fire, Hildegard is also and once again talking of her prophetic vocation. Peter got up on that first Pentecost day and declared that the disciples were not drunk as was plainly thought (Hildegard has been called crazy many times over the centuries). Rather, the disciples—read Hildegard—were fulfilling the words of the prophet Joel. Hildegard, not without reason, is appropriating these words to herself.

> In the days to come—it is the Lord who speaks—
> I will pour out my spirit on all humankind.
> Their sons and daughters shall prophesy,
> your young men shall see visions,
> your old men shall dream dreams
> even on my slaves, men and women,
> in those days I will pour out my spirit.
> (Acts 2.17, Joel 3.1-5)

Hildegard is counting herself among the recipients of this prophetic spirit.

What were the results of the Pentecost experience as recorded in Acts? "Hearing this, they were cut to the heart and said to Peter and the apostles, 'What must we do, brothers.' 'You must repent,' Peter answered." (Acts 2.37) This is the purpose of Hildegard's writings too, to cut to the heart and thus bring about metanoia or change of heart. And so her book begins. And with it all her other books and the beginning of her missionary work (the word "mission" comes from the word "to be sent") where she tells us: "Behold in the forty-third year of my temporal journey, when I grasped at a heavenly vision with great fear and trembling attention, I saw the greatest brilliance. In it a voice from heaven was saying to me: 'O weak person, you who are both ashes of ashes and decaying of decaying, speak and write what you see and hear. But you are shy about speaking and simple in explaining and unskilled about writing those things. So speak and write those things not according to human speech or human inventiveness but according to the extent that you see and hear those things in the heavens above in the marvelousness of God. Bring to light those things by way of explanation. Be like a listener who understands the words of his or her own teacher but explains them in one's own way of speaking, willingly, plainly

and instructively. So you too, o woman, speak those things which you see and hear. Write those things not according to yourself or by the standards of another person, but according to the will of the one knowing, the one who sees and arranges all things in the secrets of His own mysteries.' And a second time I heard a voice from heaven saying to me: 'Speak therefore these marvelous things and write and speak those things taught in this manner.' "[2]

It is interesting how the command is given twice to tell of the marvelous things of God—this is how the Book of Acts described the original Pentecost experience. "We hear them preaching in our language about the marvels of God," they all exclaimed. (Acts 2.11) It is also interesting how Hildegard is not claiming that her inspiration will express itself outside the limits of her own person and culture, rather her telling will be a retelling, "in one's own way of speaking." Hildegard's way will include mandalas and music, drama and preaching, Biblical as well as medical commentaries.

Hildegard's conversion can properly be described as a "Waking Up" because the image of waking from sleep is seminal to her. She says that Dabhar or the Word of God is called "word" because "by the sound of its voice the entire creation was awakened and called to itself."[3] To wake up is to be called, to know what is now and always within us. She contrasts wisdom—being awake—to foolishness—being asleep. God says: "O human being, why do you sleep? Why do you have no taste for the good works which sound in God's ears like a symphony? Who do you not search out the house of your heart."[4] Self-knowledge and awareness cannot happen unless we let go of apathy and wake up. In her first letter to the Emperor Frederick Barbarossa, Hildegard tells of a dream wherein a king "failed to open his eyes" and the result was that "a dark haze came which covered the valleys and ravens and other birds tore everything all around to pieces."[5] Hildegard herself wakes up to her own powers to communicate, to speak the truth, to critique, to lead in telling the marvelous things of God. Furthermore, Hildegard attributes the power of waking people up to the Holy Spirit in her poem: "O Holy Spirit, you make life alive, you move in all things, you are the root of all created being, you waken and reawaken everything that is."[6]

If you look carefully at the two pillars in Hildegard's self-portrait, you will be astounded to see two "stick" persons, a man on the left or red pillar and a woman on the right or green pillar. Even though I studied this picture for two years, it was only recently that a Native American, seeing it for the first time, pointed the figures out to me. They are evidently the "corn man and woman" celebrated in Hopi paintings. They are symbols of new life, of resurrection, awakening, fertility and germination.[7] For the Hopi Indians, the earth is revealed as Corn-Mother because corn "is a living entity with a body similar to man's in many respects, and the people build its flesh into their own." Implied as well in this symbol is a cycle of transmutation "involved in the process of creation itself: by his self-sacrifice the creator is dispersed or diffused throughout creation; but he may be continuously resurrected, for example, in plant form. By eating these plants men play their part in the circulation of the creator throughout the world."[8] Thus a rich symbolism of creation is present in Hildegard's very first illumination, that which tells of her own awakening, her own deepest illuminative experience. Mircea Eliade points out that the Corn-Mother imagery developed from an earlier Earth-Mother symbolism. Both are part of a "theophany of the soil," they celebrate the inexhaustible fertility of the earth, "a womb which never wearies of pro-creating."[9]

But what are Hopi images doing in a painting by a twelfth-century nun? There is much, as we shall see, in Hildegard's vision that is Native American at its roots. Perhaps this is due to the fact that both Native American and the woman's or Chothonic tradition of Germany go back to pre-patriarchal times and thus share archetypes common to matri-linear cultures. But there is another explanation as well. Some scholars believe that voyagers centuries before Columbus visited what we call the Americas.[10] These voyagers were Celts. The Celts, as we have seen, settled all along the Rhine and deeply influenced the mysticism of that area. Does it not stand to reason that they would have brought back from their distant travels symbols, stories, pictures of the wisdom they had encountered there?

The monk depicted in the picture is Hildegard's secretary, Volmar.

A

3. Viriditas: Greening Power

B

 ne of the most wonderful concepts that Hildegard gifts us with is a term that I have never found in any other theologian. She made up the word *viriditas* or greening power. Following are just a few of her celebrations of greening power. She talks of "the exquisite greening of trees and grasses," of "earth's lush greening." She says that all of creation and humanity in particular is "showered with greening refreshment, the vitality to bear fruit." Clearly creativity and greening power are intimately connected here. She says that "greening love hastens to the aid of all. With the passion of heavenly yearning, people who breathe this dew produce rich fruit." Like Eckhart, she was deeply excited by the promise in John's Gospel that we are to "bear fruit, fruit that remains." (Jn. 15.16) She believes that Christ brings "lush greenness" to "shriveled and wilted" people and institutions. She celebrates the Divine Word or Dabhar in this fashion: "The word is all verdant greening, all creativity." She calls God "the purest spring,"[1] just as Eckhart would later image God as "a great underground river." For Hildegard, the Holy

C

D

Spirit is greening power in motion, making all things grow, expand, celebrate. Indeed, for Hildegard salvation or healing is the return of greening power and moisture. She celebrates this in her opera, *Ordo Virtutum*. "In the beginning all creatures were green and vital; they flourished amidst flowers. Later the green figure itself came down." Thus Jesus is called Greenness Incarnate. "Now bear in mind," she tells us, "that the fullness you made at the beginning was not supposed to wither."[2]

What else is viriditas? It is God's freshness that humans receive in their spiritual and physical life-forces. It is the power of springtime, a germinating force, a fruitfulness that comes from God and permeates all creation. This powerful life force is found in the non-human as well as the human. "The earth sweats germinating power from its very pores," she declares. Instead of seeking body/soul in a warring struggle as did Augustine, Hildegard sees that "the soul is the freshness of the flesh, for the body grows and thrives through it just as the earth becomes fruitful through moisture."[3] Mary, the mother of Jesus, is celebrated for being the *viridissima virga*, the greenest of the green branches, the most fruitful of us all. She is a branch "full of the greening power of springtime," and in such a thought, there resound deep overtones of the goddess tradition in religion. In one of her songs to Mary she says: "You glowing, most green, verdant sprout...you bring lush greenness once more" to the "shrivelled and wilted" of the world. [4]

Where does Hildegard get this wonderful imagery? I believe from three places. First, from Scripture. The prophet Hosea writes: "I am like a cypress ever green, all your fruitfulness comes from me." (Hos. 14.9) Hildegard invokes viriditas as a synonym of blessing which is best signified to the Hebrew people as fruitfulness or creativity. As Meister Eckhart put it, "in this birth you will discover all blessing. But neglect this birth and you neglect all blessing."[5] Much of Hildegard's use of greening power stems from her meditations on the images of ourselves as vines and living branches. (cf. Jn. 15)

A second source for her rich concept of viriditas or greening power is the land where she lived. The Rhineland is a lush, voluptuously green valley, deeply blessed with rich soil, flourishing fruit and vineyards. Hildegard, we remember, spent many of her years very near the Moselle River and to this day all along her area of Bingen green vineyards lace the hills. Her Benedictine sisters still grow grapes for wine on hillsides that slope down to the river. The ambiance of greenness that characterizes the Rhineland valley is evident in the photos that accompany this text. The first photo, Photo A, is of the Nahe Valley very near the place where Hildegard spent her childhood. This river, surrounded by green, flows into the Rhine at Bingen itself. On the opposite bank of the Rhine, the rich vineyards to this day express the greening power of the soil around Bingen. The second photo, Photo B, pictures a pathway at Mount St. Disibode, the first monastery where Hildegard lived from the time she was eight years old until she was about fifty-two. It was here that she wrote *Scivias*, her first book, and with it her thirty-five visions. Isn't it appropriate that in her poem "In Honor of St. Disibode" (which she also put to music), Hildegard celebrates *his* greening power?

> *O, lifegiving greenness of God's hand,*
> *with which he has planted an orchard.*
> *You rise resplendent into the highest heavens,*
> *like a towering pillar.*
> *You are glorious in God's work.*
> *And you, o mountain heights,*
> *will never waver when God tests you.*
> *Although you stand in the distance as if in exile,*
> *No armed power is mighty enough to attack you.*
> *You are glorious in God's work.*[6]

Scientists from the University of Munich have recently been doing studies of Hildegard's cell and have found there as high an electromagnetic energy source as exists anywhere in Europe. Hildegard must have spent many sleepless nights in this cell!

In Photo C, we see the current Benedictine monastery located in Eibingen on the opposite side of the Rhine from Bingen. Hildegard started this monastery after the one at Rupertsburg and would cross the Rhine twice a week to visit it. The building you see dates back only to the nineteenth century, as the one Hildegard built was destroyed by Swedish invaders in the seventeenth century. The location depicts another example of the greening power that surrounded Hildegard constantly. And in Photo D, we are behind the current monastery and get something of a sweeping view of the Rhineland valley that Hildegard loved and knew so intimately.

The phrase "the Rhineland mystics" cannot be understood without Hildegard's term, "greening power."

The third source, then, by which Hildegard derives the term greening power, is from her own experience as a child of the Rhineland. Hildegard contrasts greening power or wetness with the sin of drying up (see Vision Twelve). A dried-up person and dried-up culture lose their ability to create. This is why drying up is so grave a sin for Hildegard—it interferes with our exalted vocation to create. "Humankind alone is called to co-create," she declares. We should be "the banner of Divinity" in this way: "God created humankind so that human-kind might cultivate the earthly and thereby create the heavenly."[7] The tragedy of drying up and ignoring greening power is that nothing is created. No doubt her deeply felt commitment to our vocation to create is related to her own "drying up," her physical and spiritual sickness that she felt from her refusal to write and to share her images. Her own resurrection and awakening was so creative an unleashing of green energy that from her forty-second year to her death at eighty-three, in music and poetry, in letter-writing and preaching, in healing and painting, in organizing and founding, Hildegard was continually creating—once she owned her own creation-centered spiritual experience. She says that we are to be co-workers with God. We are to become a flowering orchard. "The person who does good works is indeed this orchard bearing good fruit."[8] Our work is meant to be a green work, a greening work, a creative work. But to be so, it is necessary that we be as wet and moist as God. Our baptism is not a baptism *through* water but *into* moistness. It is a commitment on our part to stay wet and green. Like God.

In imagery highly reminiscent of the wisdom literature in the Hebrew Bible, Hildegard hears God speaking:

> *I am the breeze that nurtures all things green.*
> *I encourage blossoms to flourish with ripening fruits.*
> *I am the rain coming from the dew*
> *that causes the grasses to laugh*
> *with the joy of life.*[9]

We see here that laughter is not an exclusive prerogative of the two-legged ones, in Hildegard's estimation. The whole cosmos laughs. For it is wet, not dry.

4. Egg of the Universe

I n this illumination, Hildegard gifts us with a surprising and wonderful mandala of the universe—the universe as an egg. "By this supreme instrument in the figure of an egg, and which is the universe," she writes, "invisible and eternal things are manifested."[1] Where did Hildegard get the idea that the universe was egg-shaped? J.E. Cirlot comments that the concept of the Egg of the World is "a cosmic symbol which can be found in most symbolic traditions—Indian, Druidic, etc.," but that it was especially well developed in Egypt.[2] Another commentator tells us that the idea of the universe as an egg was "unusual" but not unheard of in the Middle Ages.[3] Actually, Hildegard herself was to change her opinion on the shape of the universe later in her life. By the time she wrote her last great work, *De Operatione Dei*, she had adopted the more prevalent scientific opinion of her day, namely that the universe was a sphere. No one can deny that this picture of the universe as an egg is a deeply feminine image.

There is an important lesson to be learned from this story. First, that Hildegard cares about the cosmos, cares deeply enough about it to theologize, pray, intuit, draw, and celebrate it in song, poetry, and theology. First as an egg; then as a sphere. How different this makes Hildegard from Augustine, for example, whose preoccupation with the introspective conscience of the two-legged ones and whose human chauvinism has so dominated religion and culture in the West. Instead of following Augustine, who has no cosmic Christ, and who essentially ignores nature as a source of revelation, Hildegard develops her entire theology on her own cosmology. You cannot separate God and cosmos, Christ and cosmos, humans and cosmos, in Hildegard's thought. For this reason Hildegard leaves us another lesson with this mandala. It is the importance of the work of the scientist, indeed the theological importance! She says that "all science comes from God."[4] Hildegard studied the science of her day avidly. There was not a trace of anti-intellectualism in her. In this regard she would anticipate the open intellectualism of Thomas Aquinas, who shocked the West in the next century by adopting the "pagan" Aristotle's science as a structural foundation for faith. If believers love the cosmos, then they ought to sit at the feet of those who have dedicated their lives to the holy task of examining the cosmos—that is the scientist's great contribution to culture and spirituality. In contrast to Hildegard and Aquinas, theologians of the past three hundred years have done very little studying with scientists. The sad result has been the situation best described by Otto Rank: Religion lost the cosmos in the West and society became neurotic.[5]

What is implied in Hildegard's rich image of the universe as an egg? First, an egg is a unity, a whole. This is a basic truth of the universe that Hildegard insists on time and again. She writes: "God has arranged all things in the world in consideration of everything else."[6] Just as in an egg all things are interconnected for the sake of the whole, so too in the universe. She writes: "O Holy Spirit, you are the mighty way in which every thing that is in the heavens, on the earth, and under the earth, is penetrated with connectedness, penetrated with relatedness."[7] Hildegard sees interconnectivity and interdependence as the very stuff of the universe. In this regard she would anticipate Thomas Aquinas' amazing metaphysics of relation and Meister Eckhart's observation: "The essence of everything is relation."[8] All things are penetrated with relation for Hildegard—from egg to universe; from self to other selves.

Another implication in picturing our universe as an egg is the idea of its being organic, alive, incipient. An egg is the beginning of something wonderful, a new being, a new creation. Hildegard is cele-

brating the potential of our cosmos—its hidden mysteries of delight and grandeur, of beauty and healing, as yet unrevealed. These are the "invisible and eternal things" that have yet to unfold. We humans in Hildegard's estimation, are to be instruments of that unfolding, "co-creators with God in everything we do."[9] We are the species that can reflect on the universe's laws and beauty and history to celebrate it and tell it about itself. By picturing the cosmos as an egg, Hildegard is distancing herself from Plato and all those who through the ages have envisioned the universe as essentially static. An egg is organic. The universe is in Hildegard's view an egg. Therefore the universe is organic: living, breathing, growing, surprising, renewing, loving, embracing, creating. "God gave to humankind the talent to create with all the world," she observes.[10] Hildegard calls humanity the "consummation" of the work of creation. "With nature's help, humankind can set into creation all that is necessary and life sustaining. Everything in nature, the sum total of heaven and of earth, becomes a temple and an altar for the service of God."[11]

What else is Hildegard telling us in this illumination? She envisions the universe as surrounded by a firmament of fire. "On the outer part along the circle was a bright flame. and in that fire was a globe of reddish fire so great that the entire egg was being lit up by it. Three torches were at the top."[12] The three flames at the top of the egg and the two lower down signify five planets—Saturn, Jupiter, Mars; then the sun; then Venus and Mercury; and finally the moon. The north, for Hildegard, is not at the top of the picture but on the left. The top represents the east. Thus the large flame is the sun and the mirror-like circle below the two stars signifies the moon. The winds are constantly active and depicted in four groups of triads. An inner layer contains "a certain gloomy fire so horrible that I was unable to look at it. It was shaking the entire skin with its strength, full of sounds, storms and the sharpest stones large and small." But interior from this layer of gloomy fire lay "the purest sky." Here Hildegard pictures all the stars which "serve all people" quite happily.[13] In the center of the egg, Hildegard sees "air full of water giving moisture to the entire egg." Within this circle she saw "a certain dry globe very great in size" which was practically immovable. In this globe, between the north and the east, was a mountain that separated the light from the dark. This image closely resembles a yin/yang symbol. Note that for Hildegard the earth is a sphere.

Hildegard expounds on her theological reading of this cosmic egg. She sees the outer, fiery firmament as signifying "God burning everywhere." She is truly challenging the human race to take the cosmos seriously and to quit concentrating on its chauvinistic fetishes when she says: "O humans, when the stars and the creatures were being made, where were you? Did you ever give counsel to God concerning the making of those things?"[14] Hildegard celebrates the panentheistic God who is omnipresent in things and all things in God when she declares: "I am God above all things and in all things." It is the divine goodness that permeates the cosmos in Hildegard's view. "O foolish one, who am I? Surely I am the highest good and for this reason I assign all good things to you when you have sought me carefully."[15] Hildegard sees in her cosmic vision the laws of justice and harmony that permeate the universe in balance.[16] "Those of heaven look to me and obey me according to that justice by which I have established them. They sound my praises. The sun, moon and stars appear in the clouds of heaven according to their course and the blasts of wind too and the rain in the air run as it was established for them to run. All these things are obedient to their Creator according to her command. But you, o humans, you fail to fulfill my commands. Instead you choose to follow your own will as if the justice of the law was not laid down for you and shown to you. O humans, God is just, there has arranged with a just arrangement all the things which she made in heaven and on earth."[17] Justice is built into cosmic consciousness for Hildegard as it is for the Hebrews and as for all writers of creation theology.

In her commentary on this mandala, Hildegard also praises the cosmic Christ. She equates the torch that is the sun with Christ who is "the son of justice having the lightning of burning love and existing with such glory that every creature becomes illuminated by the brightness of his light."[18] Christ is mid-way between the heavenly planets and the earth in the mandala for he comes *from* heaven but *to* the earth. He enters the colder atmosphere of the earth, "bent compassionately in the direction of the poverty of the human race, sustaining many hard-

ships by hastening very many sufferings to himself when he showed himself in a physical way to the world." Hildegard also symbolizes in this cosmic mandala the church as the moon. Because it "has not been founded in itself, but is dependent upon Christ," it is like the moon to the sun. The church at its best "shines white in the faith of innocent brightness and holds out great honor." The two torches above the moon now signify the Bible with its Old Testament and its New Testament. The three winds signify the preaching of the Good News on the one hand and the sacrament of baptism on the other. Faith is spread by those two means. Baptism corresponds to the moisture that permeates the entire egg. "Baptism brought to the entire world the water of salvation to those who believe. From time to time it suddenly gathers itself together and then sends forth an unexpected rain with much crashing. At other times it spreads itself out softly and lends a caressing rain with gentle breezes." Baptism and faith are spread by the prophets "for the healing of people who are touched by them."

Thus Hildegard has woven together in this one amazing mandala the entire cosmology of her time: earth, air, fire, water were considered the basic elements of the universe, and they were understood to constitute the essential elements of the human body in her day as well. Her vision awakens us to our deep relationship with all that God has made. She challenges us to make a synthesis equally compelling and wonderful of the cosmic elements that our generation believes in—and to weave it as beautifully and energetically into a picture of wholeness and interaction, of microcosm and macrocosm.

I was once sharing this mandala with a group of students and asked them their personal response to it without having shared with them anything Hildegard said about it. One student replied: "I see a nest." A nest is a striking way to name our cosmos and our relation to it. The universe is indeed our home, our nest. If we truly saw it that way, would we tolerate a fouling of that nest? Would we accept disruption of the nest that human folly— injustice, war, pollution, nuclear madness—leads to? Or would we treat the nest, our home, with the compassion and reverence, respect and justice, that Hildegard calls for?

5. The Cosmic Wheel

he next three illuminations are not from Hildegard's first book, *Scivias*, but from one written twenty-eight years later, *De Opera-tione Dei* (On the Work of God). She tells us that she is trying in these pictures to carry on her image of the universe as an egg. Only this time, because the latest science told her so, the universe is pictured as an un-egg-like sphere. She sees "a wheel of marvelous appearance visible right in the center of the breast" of a towering figure.[1] In picturing the cosmos as a wheel, Hildegard is not only talking of its spherical shape (which is what scientists in her day were saying of its movement), she is celebrating a spiral or moving wheel image for the universe. The figure in the wheel's center with arms extended like a cross is named the mystic center of the cosmos. "Like the Tree of Life, the cross stands for the 'world-axis,' " Cirlot points out.[2]

Who is the figure holding the wheel to his/her chest? It is "a wondrously beautiful image within the mystery of God. It had a human form, and its countenance was of such beauty and radiance that I could have more easily gazed at the sun than at that face."[3] Who is the figure? ". . . Love appearing in a human form, the Love of our heavenly Father. . . Love—in the power of the everlasting Godhead, full of exquisite beauty, marvelous in its mysterious gifts."[4] The figure speaks to Hildegard, saying: "I, the highest and fiery power, have kindled every spark of life, and I emit nothing that is deadly. I decide on all reality. With my lofty wings I fly above the globe. With wisdom I have rightly put the universe in order. I, the fiery life of divine essence, am aflame beyond the beauty of the meadows. I gleam in the waters. I burn in the sun, moon and stars. With every breeze, as with invisible life that contains everything, I awaken everything to life."[5] The Creator and wisdom figure of the Godhead is also keeper of cosmic justice. "I have established pillars that sustain the entire globe."

Hildegard explains how this present vision compares to that of the universe as egg. First, the entire cosmos now rests within the bosom of the Creator—this is panentheism as it has never been pictured before or since! The universe as God's womb, the egg becoming an organism, expressive and alive. The cosmos is still surrounded by "luminous fire" on the outside and by "black fire" on the inside and by a watery air that "moistens all the other circles with dampness."[6]

In the center of the giant wheel there is a human figure with the crown of its head projected upward, "while the feet touch a sphere of sheer white luminous air." The fingertips of left and right hands are extended, "forming a cross extending to the circumference of the circle." In what Hildegard calls the "cosmic wheel" are the heads of animals breathing onto the human figure: leopard, wolf, lion, bear, stag, crab, serpent, and lamb. Seven planets exist in the various circles and "all the planets shone their rays at the animal heads as well as at the human figure." Sixteen major stars appear within the circle and other, lesser, stars fill the circles of air. The Godhead that Hildegard describes, though it is pictured in masculine form, speaks loudly of maternity. She writes: "Just as a wheel encloses within itself what lies hidden within it, so also does the Holy Godhead enclose everything within itself without limitation, and it exceeds everything." Another richly panentheistic image!

It is difficult to imagine a more ecological revelation than Hildegard offers us here: "God has composed the world out of its elements for the glory of his name. He has strengthened it with the winds, bound and illuminated it with the stars, and filled it with the other creatures. On this world he has surrounded and strengthened human beings with all these things and steeped them in very great power so that all creation supports the human race in all things. All nature ought to be at the service of human beings so that they can work with nature since, in fact, human beings can neither live nor survive without it." Hildegard is not only talking *about* interdependence, she is inviting us *into* the hospitable cosmos that will befriend humankind and lend us its very great power. But as guests we need to acknowledge how thoroughly we depend upon nature for survival and blessing. Hildegard promises: "This will be shown to you in this vision." In other words, our interdependence with nature will shine forth within if we pray this mandala rightly.

Hildegard introduces her meditation on the human figure by citing a passage from Paul where he promises that "you will shine in the world like bright stars because you are offering it the word of life." (Phil. 2.16) How does Hildegard interpret the human figure in this vision? She is now expounding on the relation of microcosm/macrocosm, the moral responsibility that interdependence demands of us. We have in the following meditation from Hildegard a profound summary of the theology of the royal person—a celebration of our beauty and a challenge to live up to it by creativity, leadership, and justice-making. She says: "Humanity stands in the midst of the structure of the world. For it is more important than all other creatures which remain dependent on that world. Although small in stature, humanity is powerful in the power of its soul. Its head is turned upward and its feet toward the solid ground, and it can place into motion both the higher and the lower things. Whatever it does with its deed in the right or the left hand permeates the universe, because in the power of its inner humanity it has the potential to accomplish such things. Just as, for example, the body of a human being exceeds the heart in size, so also are the powers of the soul more powerful than those of the body. . . .The powers of the soul extend over the entire globe."[7] We look constantly at other creatures, Hildegard observes, yet "it is God whom human beings know in every creature. For they know that God is the Creator of the whole world." How beautifully, how freely, how magnificently Hildegard invites us to let go of human chauvinism. God is in every creature—not just the two-legged ones, much less the baptized ones of our race. The cosmos is truly a temple.

Hildegard considers the animal figures in this mandala to stand for "powers of virtue" that keep humanity going and working in the universe. Thus, for example, the stag stands for faith and holiness. When humans experience suffering we are "like a bear in bodily pain" which cannot get rid of its pain but teaches us an "inner meekness, causing us to walk along the right path by exercising patience like a lamb and to avoid evil by behaving as cleverly as a serpent. For through the distress of the body we often attain spiritual treasures through which we come into possession of a higher kingdom."[8] Virtues for Hildegard are powers that humans exert on the cosmos. They are as diverse as the various species that people the universe.

Finally, Hildegard's meditation returns to the love that permeates the cosmos, the love of the Creator who embraces the cosmos and holds the universe in her breast. "Out of the original source of the true Love in whose knowledge the cosmic wheel rests, there shines forth an exceedingly precise order over all things. And this order which preserves and nourishes everything comes to light in a way that is ever new. . .It is Love which here properly distinguishes and moderately adapts the powers of the elements and of the other lofty adornment associated with the strength and beauty of the world as well as with the entire physical structure of humanity. . . . Out of this true love, which is totally divine, there arises all goodness, which is to be desired above everything else. Love draws to itself all who desire God, and with this impulse Love goes to meet them."[9] Thus does Hildegard celebrate the true invitation of the cosmos: personalized in the Godhead, beloved like a fetus in the womb, creative to the point of birthing all creatures with divine faces, and generous to have birthed humanity a lover after its own most primordial origin and source. From love to love—that is the human journey—spiritual and cosmic, physical and divine.

We make the journey within the circle and embrace of the Godhead that "embraces all."[10] For "in this circle of earthly existence you shine so finely, it surpasses understanding. God hugs you. You are encircled by the arms of the mystery of God."[11]

6. The Human as Microcosm of the Macrocosm

ildegard entitles her reflections on Vision Six: "On Human Nature."[1] Yet one can see readily that she has much more in mind than humanity in this vision— she has the cosmos in mind and she offers a "close-up" of the human (microcosm)/ cosmic (macrocosm) relationship. The human body, for Hildegard, is in the cosmos and the cosmos is in the human body. One forms the other. "Now God has built the human form into the world structure, indeed even the cosmos, just as an artist would use a particular pattern in his or her work."[2]

In commenting on this image, Hildegard emphasizes the role of the winds in affecting human health and balance, whether moral, psychological, or physical. "I looked—and behold!—the east wind and the south wind, together with their sidewinds, set the firmament in motion with powerful gusts, causing the firmament to rotate around the earth from East to West." The winds, she believed, affected the human body profoundly. "I notice how the humors in the human organism are disturbed and altered by various qualities of the winds and air. . .The wind affects human beings. . . .Sometimes the alteration may weaken individuals, and at other times it strengthens them."

Hildegard is concerned about the winds because of the understanding that breath and spirit come from the same root word. Body and soul are affected by the air we breathe and the manner in which we breathe it. She speaks of our inhaling and exhaling this "breath of the world"—another instance of the universe as an organism, a single, breathing, living body. "If we human beings whose natural disposition may correspond to that breath of the world inhale this altered air and exhale it once again so that the soul can receive this breath and carry it even further into the body's interior, then the humors of our organism are altered."

What is most useful to us in these visions of Hildegard is her immense respect for the whole, for the interconnections of parts, for the harmony of humanity and cosmos. As Heinrich Schipperges puts it, "the subject of these visions [Visions Five, Six, Seven in the present book] is the unity of the order of creation, which includes the world of angels and the world of nature, one world in plants, animals, and human beings, a single world in the life of the senses, soul, and grace. Nature and grace, body and spirit, body and soul, world and the church—everything is in harmony and glorifies unanimously the Creator."[3] What is most important is that Hildegard constructs medicine and morality on cosmology. To recover a sense of *micro/macro* is no small deed, no exercise in abstraction. The way we build our lives, our culture, our physical and psychological world must be one with the universe. We must take our *moral living* from the universe and not the other way around. Again we have here a rich instance of Hildegard's rejection of anthropomorphism. Humanity derives beauty for creativity not from isolation but from the universe itself.

Schipperges describes Hildegard's sense of culture and cosmos in the following: "[For Hildegard] the world means all natural phenomena and also the whole phenomenon of civilization. In both these areas Hildegard learns about the *numinosum* and *fascinosum* of God's rule in the world, the *operatio Dei* (the work of God)." The work of God, we recall, is the very title of the book from which we are deriving Visions Five, Six, and Seven. Hildegard is saying that the work of God *is* the work of the cosmos. More explicitly, God's work, is microcosm (humanity) and macrocosm (universe) working and creating together. There is no dualism here. There is no put-down of what philosophers like Aquinas would later celebrate as "secondary causes." There is here a basic principle for welcoming evolution as not denigrating the work of God but actually revealing a more intimate presence in cosmic history than we had dreamed possible.

Schipperges says Hildegard "experiences as numinous all things in natural creation: fire and water, clouds and streams, stars and winds and storms, the moon and the night, a fountain and a meadow, as well as the sinister regions of an uninhabitable earth. All civilization on earth is fascinating: the ploughing and harvesting of fields, the construction of a house and the shaping of a vessel, the work of a smith and the creation of an artist, the thriving of earthly activity and all threats as a result of failure, the terror of guilt and the quagmire of sin— and day-by-day and hour-by-hour, the inevitable decision making of human beings in all their actions."[4] Here we have for certain an ecological morality and the basis for a sense of salvation as healing—physical, psychological, social, and spiritual healing. Her morality is not built on guilt or on compulsions of a 'moral imperative' but on relationship—cosmic relating, not merely two-legged relating.

In keeping with her effort to relate all the spheres of reality, Hildegard imagines the winds and humors of our bodies as animals. The leopard "roars wildly within us and at other times more calmly." Some humors "crawl forward or backward like a crab, signifying in this way our changeability." Some behave like a stag "whose leaping thrusts are a sign of contradiction." Others have "the predatory nature of a wolf" or a lion "that wishes to show off its inconquerable power." How interesting that Hildegard often pictures the serpent in a favorable light—it "can be either gentle or angry." In this, as in many other instances, Hildegard reveals the influence of the ancient goddess religions wherein the snake was a source of energy and wisdom rather than a temptress. Sometimes the winds and the humors appear "as mild as a lamb" or they may "growl within us like an angry bear."[5]

The breath that humans breathe is not only cosmic but divine. There lies our strength—found in "divine might." Such power "strengthens in every limb the inner sense of those who bind themselves to God." With the breath of God that touches us, we inhale "the mysterious gifts of the Holy Spirit" which arouse us from dullness and boredom. What are we awakened to? "We shall awaken from our dullness and arise vigorously toward justice."[6] Boredom and apathy, carelessness and listlessness— Hildegard says that these come from two sources: shutting ourselves off from cosmic relationships and ignoring injustice. Thomas Aquinas in the next century would attribute acedia or spiritual boredom to forgetfulness of our divinity. Hildegard writes, "The God who has created me is also my own power because without God I am unable to do any good deed and because I have only through God the living spirit through which I live and am moved, through which I learn to know all my ways." In celebrating humanity's divinization, Hildegarde acknowledges the moral responsibilities and the immense dignity that go with it. Wakefulness to cosmos and to justice produces trust. "For just as the sun is fixed in the firmament of heaven and has power over the creatures of the earth so that nothing can overcome them, so also believers who have their hearts and minds directed toward God cannot be forgotten by God."[7] We are to ingest the sun, the fiery divinity that surrounds the cosmos. "Are we not all the more inflamed in our blissful effort because formerly we burned for what was good? We dwell already on those lofty places where we remain in full rapture and the greatest longing. Our power exceeds the firmament and extends to the bottom of the abyss because humanity in the midst of creation is exceedingly strong. And the whole world is at our service."[8] Once we begin to see how cosmic we are, our whole world opens up for us. Our greatness and our beauty; our responsibility and the meaning of our decision making take on cosmic dimensions.

This mandala moves Hildegard to discourse on health or illness in the human body. It is interesting and "useful" (using her word) to note that the key word in this section is "justice." We who have been deprived of a sense of cosmos in our science and religion and medicine are surprised to read so much about justice in a treatise on health. But a cosmic consciousness is necessarily a justice consciousness, as I have pointed out elsewhere.[9] Why? Because the universe itself works by laws of harmony and balance, that is by way of justice. Justice is not a moral virtue, an ethical norm as humans conceive; it is an operative pattern by which the universe holds together and is symmetrically bound. Because of justice the universe survives and thrives. Humans are invited to enter the pattern which exists everywhere we look, including our own bodies. In this section Hildegard talks of the need for strength which comes "through the virtuous power of a proper equilibrium."[10] When that happens "we shall rejoice and be merry." Hildegard celebrates the balance, harmony, and joy that justice brings to one's own or society's healing. "When the salvation of good and just people is progressing favorably, justice is active through the Holy Spirit so that such people rise up in victory to God and accomplish good deeds."[11] To make justice happen within and around us we need self-discipline. "Self-discipline is an accumulation of the strengths and preserving powers of justice." Such discipline comes from discretion and avoids scrupulosity. It requires a "gentleness of spirit and prudence." The just path is one "of reverent discipline."[12] Reverence requires openness, and only through openness can justice exist. "For if our thoughts grow opinionated and obdurate and enter in this way onto empty byways, we shall oppress justice as a result. It is justice which, when sprinkled by the dew of the Holy Spirit, ought to germinate good works through holiness."[13] Self-discipline renders us moist and open to being sprinkled still more by the Holy Spirit. We succumb to dryness and "lack an infusion of heavenly dew" and our souls "waste away" when we ignore this lesson.[14] And we become instruments of injustice.

Hildegard tells of a voice *giving her*, in light of this mandala, the following message: "God has directed for humanity's benefit all of creation, which God has formed both on the heights and in the depths. But if we abuse our condition and commit evil deeds, then God's justice will allow other creatures to punish us."[15] The abuse of the land or the waters, the air or the atomic powers of the universe, will lead to the just punishment of the species that has heaped that abuse. Love Canal, Times Beach, Three Mile Island—all these instances bear out Hildegard's prophetic warning. Justice is not rained down from above by a vengeful God—rather it comes from the web of creation itself. The interconnectivity of creation and humanity demands justice. The fields will no longer yield their fruit where human greed and injustice have sought too quick a yield and have poisoned the earth with excessive chemicals. All this is cosmic justice responding to human injustice.

How do humans remain healthy? By balance, by justice. We are to "harmonize well" with God, creation, others, and self. When we do this our joy will be "like the sunrise. You display to all other people a wondrously beautiful mode of life patterned after the way of the Son of God." This pattern of justice and compassion cannot be contained. It will flow into all your creativity and all your work because it comes from so deep a center and source in yourself. "At this point your soul is called a prince's daughter—the daughter of the One who is called 'Prince of Peace.' " Thus, we become others' Christs. The cosmic Christ and the mystical body of Christ find their incarnation in us and in our life's work. And we become instruments of divine peace which, after all, is what the Incarnation was all about. "The angels announced peace to humanity at the Incarnation of the Son of God." With the peace comes "sheer joy," because God and humanity are wedded by creation. "The Incarnation was the cause of sheer joy since God had bound himself to earth in such a way that human beings could behold him in human form, while the angels could gaze on him perfectly as both man and God."[16] Here, at the end of her commentary on this vision, we see how Hildegard sees more than one person in her mandala of microcosm/macrocosm. She sees here the New Adam, the new Everyman and Everywoman, the Cosmic Christ, the Mystical Body of Christ, you and me, all Christs in our deepest depths. And she sees the peace and joy that are a cosmic peace and joy that was promised at the first Christmas when, we were told, heaven and earth, angels and shepherds, beheld an amazing coming together: that of Divinity and humanity.

7. Cultivating the Cosmic Tree

n this beautiful mandala and her commentary on it, Hildegard celebrates the deep psychological healing that occurs when microcosm and macrocosm are wedded again. We see in this cosmic wheel humans cultivating the earth through the seasons of the year and the seasons of their lives. Here the previous two mandalas, "The Cosmic Wheel" and "The Human as Microcosm of the Macrocosm," find their fulfillment. Human creativity and gentle but industrious cultivating of the earth is what the cosmos longs to see and has longed to birth during twenty billion years of history. Why has Hildegard chosen the tree as the symbol of the cosmos at play? J.E. Cirlot comments on the meaning of the tree in symbolic history. "In its most general sense, the symbolism of the tree denotes the life of the cosmos: its consistence, growth, prolifera-tion, generative and regenerative processes. It stands for inexhaustible life."[1]

Hildegard was truly celebrating life with this vision, for she says "God is life."[2] She knows this from observing the divine brilliance in creatures. "All living creatures are, so to speak, sparks from the radiation of God's brilliance, and these sparks emerge from God like the rays of the sun." She asks a necessary question: "How would God be known as life if not through the fact that the realm of the living, which glorifies and praises God also emerges from God? On this account God has established the living, burning sparks as a sign of the brilliance of the divine renown." The fiery firmament is a footstool to the throne of God and all creatures are sparks from this fire. We sparks come from God. "But if God did not give off these sparks, how would the divine flame become fully visible? And how would God be known as the Eternal One if no brilliance emerged from God? For no creature exists that lacks a radiance— be it greenness or seed, buds or beauty. Otherwise it would not be a creature at all."[3] Every being is holy, every being is beautiful, every being is radiant, every being shares a spark of the divine fire. Here we have a theological locus for Meister Eckhart's image of the *ancilla animae*, the spark of the soul, that all humans possess. To be a creature for Hildegard is to be brilliant, beautiful, and on fire with the heavenly flame.

Hildegard's trees reveal roots, trunk, and foliage. Eliade believes that the tree symbolizes "the center of the world" expressed in terms of a world-axis. This world-axis symbolism, like so much in Hildegard's work, goes back to pre-Neolithic times. The tree symbolizes at the same time "the central point in the cosmos" and human nature itself "which follows on the equation of the macrocosm with the microcosm."[4] Hildegard celebrates in this vision once again the fertility of the earth. "I saw how moisture from the gentle layer of air flowed over the earth. This air revived the earth's greening power and caused all fruits to put forth seeds and become fertile. . . . From the gentle layer of air, moisture effervesces over the earth. This awakens the earth's greenness and causes all fruits to appear through germination."[5] One can see in this vision how dominant the waters are in Hildegard's picture of creativity. This is why staying wet and moist are such important virtues to Hildegard—without the moisture there is no creativity, no fertility.

In this vision Hildegard emphasizes psychological healing and regeneration. She celebrates a fruitful mutuality between body and soul when she writes: "Our inner spirit so announces our power in both earthly and heavenly matters that even our body can foster an intimate association in its creative power with these things. For wherever soul and body live together in proper agreement, they attain the highest reward in mutual joy." When she speaks of sexual organs in this and the previous vision, she invariably uses the term "reverence." Just as the human head is round, so is the firmament and so is the human soul. Justice and symmetry are the soul's quest. "The soul displays in its essence both roundness and symmetry."[6] There is a symmetrical balance that the

psyche or soul seeks. For when we sin, the soul "will then renew itself contritely in justice. Thus the soul displays symmetry because, even though it has delighted in sinning, it has then become disturbed in sorrow. And so the soul maintains a reverent attitude as well as firmness in its reverence." It is this "reverence within our soul" that overcomes evil. Hildegard compares sin to indigestion, and even with daily habits of sinning "our soul can still illuminate our body. . . .Thus, in the midst of contradictions, we accomplish both good and evil." Sin for Hildegard is an acquiescence to a loss of balance, to injustice. But justice is a cosmic gift. "God has formed humanity according to the model of the firmament and strengthened human power with the might of the elements. God has firmly adapted the powers of the world to us so that we breathe, inhale, and exhale these powers like the sun, which illuminates the earth, sends forth its rays, and draws them back again to itself." When body and soul work together to carry out good deeds, then "the soul will bring joy to the body." One example dear to Hildegard of soul bringing joy to body (working in consort with wind and breath) is singing. Anyone who has sung the demanding music that Hildegard composed is aware how serious she was about celebrating cosmic inhaling and exhaling.

Tears of repentance Hildegard sees as further evidence of the cosmic moisture that brings greening life force back to nature and human relationships. From "sighs and tears of humble repentance" the body acquires strength for virtuous works. What Hildegard envisions in this mandala is the great work of humanity and creation cooperating; body and soul, water and Earth come together to bear fruit. For Hildegard, the cosmic tree and the world axis do not just sit there. They require cultivation and human creativity. The world is organic, but human ingenuity is required to bring the organism to its full potential.

She compares the cyclic turn of the seasons to a potter's wheel. "The sun's heat and the moisture of the waters cultivate the whole earth, make it fruitful, and complete it, just as a potter completes his vessels by turning his wheel."[6] She envisions this wheel of the earth as a potter's wheel bearing fruit. We are told by Cirlot that in the alchemical tradition, of which Hildegard was not ignorant, a tree with suns symbolized the solar *opus,* the Great Work. The expression "to plant the philosophers' tree" means to stimulate the creative imagination.[7] Surely Hildegard is celebrating the birth of wisdom that comes with creativity in this mandala. Creativity is a cosmic as well as a human power. Her allusion to the seven planets together with the tree in this wheel is an allusion to prime matter, that empty potential from which all things arise. This may explain why she also discourses in this section on how "light is honored by darkness, and the darker part serves the lighter part."[8] Humans have empty spaces as well as full ones in them, as does the cosmos. The via negativa (emptiness) is essential for the via creativa (birthing).

When we put moisture and heat together with earth and fire, wisdom is born. "The power of human virtue is fulfilled in the fire of the Holy Spirit and the moisture of humility within the vessel of the Holy Spirit, where Wisdom has made her abode."[9] Clearly the elements of earth, air, fire, water are all being celebrated by Hildegard in this mandala. But they are celebrated now within the context of human creativity and specifically within the image of a potter at work on his or her wheel. Here lies wisdom for Hildegard, in the very act of birthing and creativity and intercommunion with the forces of the universe. Here is the abode where wisdom dwells. It is also the presence of God: the Shekinah where wisdom has set up her tent. Wisdom, she writes, "resides in all creative works."[10]

Hildegard completes her meditation on the cosmic tree with a lengthy exegesis of the first chapter of John's Gospel. There we are reminded that the light of God came into the world (Hildegard might prefer spark or fire or flame of God) to set its tent among us. (Jn. 1.14). One more creative and divine act in an already lavishly abundant divine cosmos. The divine Word, the incarnation of divine wisdom itself, "took on human flesh in his humanity" in order to bring "all creation to the light."[11] But to be called to light and to Word is to be called to our divine origins, which means creativity. Our divinity is our creativity. We are to play an active role on the cosmic potter's wheel. For, according to Hildegard, the cosmic wheel cannot turn and accomplish its purpose if humanity's creativity does not enter lustfully into the work.

49

8. The Creator's Glory, Creation's Glory

n the previous four mandalas we saw how fire permeates the universe of Hildegard. In this picture cosmic fire enters more directly into the human sphere. Here, God the Creator sits on a throne and his footstool is fire. Yet the footstool appears in the form of a shell. The shell was a common symbol in the Middle Ages for quenching of thirst. It serves as a reminder of water as a source of fertility. Eliade teaches that the shell is also related to the moon and to woman as in the story of the birth of Aphrodite from a shell. The fiery footstool, as shell, sits on a pool of water. I feel the earth celebrated as water, as creative place, as womb, in this picture. The blue earth resembles the pictures taken from space in our time showing the whole, beautiful, creative mandala we call home. The round mandala of living water bespeaks the fetal waters of Mary's womb and also symbolizes Christ offering "living waters" for those who thirst after justice. Hildegard stresses the role justice plays when commenting on the Creator image in this picture. One is also reminded of the prophet who said that in the Messianic times "justice will flow like a river."

The color gold dominates this picture and Hildegard tells us why. She sees "a royal throne with a circle around it on which there was sitting a certain living person full of light of wondrous glory. . . . And from this person so full of light sitting on the throne there extended out a great circle of gold color as from the rising sun. I was in no way able to grasp its fullness. It spread itself in every direction upwards into the height of heaven and downwards into the depth of the abyss. I could see no end to it."[1] Gold, the color of royalty and divinity, permeates the entire universe as does Divinity itself.

In naming the watery wheel as the abyss, Hildegard may be making another association with the Great Mother and earth-god cults. "The abyss is usually identified with the 'land of the dead,' the under-world, and is hence, though not always, associated with the Great Mother and earth-god cults," notes Cirlot.[2] Who is this resplendent royal person? "This is the living God, ruling over all things, shining bright in goodness and with wondrous things in his works, whose immeasurable brightness in the depths of his mystery no single person can gaze at perfectly."[3] Hildegard is connecting us to the rich theology of the royal persons of the Hebrew Bible. In this theology God is celebrated as Creator, leader, healer and justice-maker of the cosmos.[4] The gold signifies God's wonderful presence and the powerful work that never ceases in creation.

Hildegard was commanded to tell a story about this image. "I heard him say to me: 'O how beautiful your eyes are when you tell the divine story! How the dawn arises in your eyes when you tell the divine plan!"[5] What is the story Hildegard has to tell? It is about the goodness of creation and the Creator. "Now write about the true knowledge of the Creator in his goodness," she is commanded. The story concerns how "God, who created all things, ordained humans for glory." The gold that emanates from the divine person wants to penetrate into humanity. The royal personhood seeks a human home, the Divine yearns to dwell in the human. God sits on a throne; thus God is at rest. God wants to be at rest, seated in the human mind where wisdom is stored. Neither power nor mastery will grasp God, but faith and wisdom will. Thus Hildegard tells us that "every faithful soul is a throne of God if it reverences God wisely." The symbol of the seat of God or throne of God signifies "the center. . .synthesis, stability and unity."[6] If we live wisely, Hildegard says, God is at our center, God is centered in us. Indeed, the axis or center of the cosmos is found at that juncture. Divinity enthroned, glory exuded, justice shared, wisdom seated. But understand that *all* persons are capable of being such centers of Divinity, homes for God.

No doubt Hildegard is making use of some of the extremely rich Biblical imagery about the royal power of God in this picture. Yahweh, the Bible says, is enthroned and has the ark of the covenant as his footstool (1 Ch. 28.2; Ps. 99.5; 132.7); or, Sion is his footstool (Lam. 2.1) or the whole earth is God's footstool (Is. 66.1; Mt. 5.35; Acts 7.49). Hildegard, saturated in the Psalms, is evidently drawing on psalmic imagery in this picture. I heartily recommend reading the following psalms while being with Hildegard's picture: 99, 110, and 132. In these psalms are found all the themes Hildegard writes about in her commentary on this image. Especially that of the royal dignity of creation: "Royal dignity was yours from the day you were born, on the holy mountains, royal from the womb, from the dawn of your earliest days." (110.3) God's throne is established forever (Ps. 32.2) and is a throne of grace (Heb. 4.16). Hildegard's picturing of the universe bathed in gold is her way of celebrating creation's glory, the presence of God throughout creation. "God has made heaven and earth in great glory," she writes.[7] She understands creation to have been birthed out of God's pleasure. "God the Father had such delight in himself that he called forth the whole creation through his Word. And then his creation pleased him too and every creature that he lovingly touched, he took in his arms. O, what great delight you have in your work!"[8]

Just as a feminine symbol, that of the shell and of water, enters this picture of creation, so does a "Lady" enter Hildegard's fuller story of creation. In a letter to Abbot Adam of Ebrach, Hildegard reports seeing in a vision "an extraordinarily beautiful young woman. . .wearing shoes which seemed of purest gold [whom] the whole creation called 'Lady.' " The image spoke to a human person of sapphire blue (cf. Vision One above) and said: "Dominion is yours on the day of your power in the radiance of the saints. I have brought you forth from my own womb before the daystar." And then Hildegard heard a voice tell her, "The young woman whom you see is Love. She has her tent in eternity. For when God wanted to create the world, he bent down with the most tender love. He provided for everything that was necessary, just like a father who prepares an inheritance for his child and with the zeal of loves makes all his possessions available. . . . For it was love which was the source of this creation in the beginning when God said: 'Let it be!' And it was. As though in the blinking of an eye, the whole creation was formed through love." Continuing her story, Hildegard celebrates Psalm 110, "The right hand of God embraces all creatures and is especially extended over peoples, kingdoms, and all goods. And that is why it stands written in the scripture: 'The Lord says to my lord: "Sit at my right hand." ' " But why does the whole creation call this maiden "Lady"? Because "it was from her that all creation proceeded, since love was the first. She made everything." This is an astounding and exciting statement from Hildegard— that womanly love birthed all creation. She elaborates. "Love created humankind. . . .Love was in eternity and it brought forth in the beginning of all holiness all creatures without any admixture of evil."[9] The gold and glory in this illumination permeates *all* of creation, not just *human* creation. Hildegard says "no creature, whether visible or invisible, lacks a spiritual life." Why is this so? Because "it is written: 'The Spirit of the Lord fills the earth.' "[10]

The Creator God pictured here is a God who loves justice. "God is bright justice which has no trace of injustice." Thus God never calls injustice just and is displeased by those who do. The Creator God "is that justice which, like steel, strengthens all the rest of justice. . . . He is the judicial fire that burns every sin of injustice."[11] Part of the fire imagery in this picture, then, is the purging motif that true justice brings. This God exists "like a flame and enkindles and sets fire and illuminates all things." There is no end in the entire cosmos to the "power and work and justice of God." Justice always accompanies God's power and work. We cannot escape justice in the abyss and cannot escape it in heaven. We sin when we "who ought to bear the burning fruit of justice do not bear it" and the prophet Ezekiel warned of this when he wrote: "Behold I will kindle a fire in you, and I will burn up in you all greenwood and all dry wood." The justice of God wants to "flame in the hearts of the faithful ones." Hildegard ends this meditation with a hint that perhaps the blue circle which is a moving, turning circle represents the coming of Christ into our midst. Are the blue, swirling fetal waters going to become a man in sapphire blue? Are womb and compassion related? She talks of how in the womb of the Virgin the spoils and plundering of the devil were destroyed.

If you look closely you can see little rib-like lines on the edges of the footstool and the watery circle. Perhaps Hildegard has in mind that recent invention of her day, the windmill. She talks about this invention in her writings. If so, she is saying that fire and water, divine footstool and watery earth, are interconnected like mechanical parts. Together they make the world go round and we cannot separate one from the other. Moreover, the windmill raises water, great amounts of it, to the surface. That is the work of Mary and her Son: to bring the waters of wisdom and justice to play once again that they might flood the earth. Was it not Christ who spoke of a baptism by fire as well as a baptism by water?

9. Original Blessing: The Golden Tent

 n this vision Hildegard begins to name the human journey specifically. The divine gold that we saw celebrated in the previous picture now takes on a four-sided form, a symbol for the wisdom of God, as it enters the womb which in turn enters the body of the baby fetus. Hildegard calls this "golden tent" or golden kite—such a rich symbol of royal personhood— the "king-dom of God."[1] We are heirs of divinity, of regal wisdom and beauty. Notice that within the four-sided symbol for Divinity there is a three-part division. Thus we have Divinity represented here both as quarternity and as Trinity—a rare instance in Christian lore of such imaging. Carl Jung believes that only a woman could have come up with the idea of representing God as four-sided, thus including earth as an integral part of Divinity.[2] Hildegard herself reminds us that the four sides of this kite represent the four points of the cosmos—our inheri-tance is a cosmic gift. "I saw the greatest and most serene brightness, like a flame with very many eyes, and having four corners turned to the four parts of the world."[3] This means, she points out, "the great knowledge of God in mysteries and the pure knowledge of God in manifestations which extend a radiance of great depth of clarity and sharp edges of fourfold stability to the four regions of the world. The mystery or celestial majesty foresees most keenly both those who are rejected and those who are brought together."[4] God's eyes see the pain of the world and the joy of the world. Thus Hildegard presents on two sides of her kite what she calls "countless eyes" which signify God's seeing and knowing. In the Book of Zechariah we are told that the seven eyes of God "run to and fro through the whole earth." (Zech. 4.10)

In the center of the golden kite are little red balls which Hildegard calls "burning spheres" or "fireballs." She says: "A fireball possesses the heart of this child. Because the soul, burning with the fire of deep understanding and not having the form of human members, discerns different things in its journey of understanding. The fireball is neither flesh nor fallen like the body of a person. It comforts the heart of the human being because it exists so to speak like the foundation of the body. It rules the en-tire body just as the firmament of heaven contains lowly things and covers celestial things and also touches the brain of the person. The fireball tastes not only earthly but also heavenly things with its powers when it knows God wisely. It pours itself through all the limbs of the person and gives the greenness of the heart and veins and all the organs to the entire body as a tree gives sap and greenness to all the branches from its root."[5] Today, cosmologist Brian Swimme teaches that the original fireball which began all of creation twenty billion years ago is literally present in our brains when photons go off, and in the process of photosynthesis, or what Hildegard describes as the greening of the plants.[6] Hildegard says in her fashion that the sun's energy makes these things happen on earth.

It is especially important to link this reflection of fireballs entering the soul of the living person with the previous picture of sparks from God's fiery footstool flying down to all creatures. Hildegard is showing us in this image how she sees fire transmitted to humans. In my opinion this synchronicity between a twelfth century mystic and a twentieth century physicist is one of the obvious examples of how Hildegard did not *know* all that she was saying; in other words, her writing and visioning were truer than her conscious awareness could articulate.

Hildegard reflects on the scene of the golden kite which is itself in an egg-like shape, symbolizing the microcosm being born in the macrocosm (remember at this time she still believed the universe to be egg-shaped as in Vision Four above). She sees "a woman having the whole form of a person in her womb. This happens because after the woman has taken in the human seed an infant is formed in the fullness of its limbs in the secret chamber of her womb. Behold, through the hidden plan of the heavenly Creator, the same form gives the movement that begins life. By a secret and hidden order from the will of God, the infant in a mother's womb received by an appropriate divine order a spirit, and always at the right time. It shows it has life by moving its body just like the earth that reveals itself by bringing forth the flowers of its fruit when the dew falls on it."[7] Hildegard plays with the Trinitarian symbol within the kite, at times seeing it as standing for the trinity of the soul—understanding, reason and will; and at times seeing it stand for the trinity of the human person—soul, body and senses. But mostly she discourses in this section on the Trinity of the Father, Son, and Holy Spirit. She is saying that the Divine Personhood truly enters the soul at birth. It enters the body too, for she refers to the kite as soul and also as body. What could be a fuller celebration of our original blessing, our royal personhood, our divine origin, than this picture by Hildegard of our holy birth?

Even though Hildegard celebrates the glorious divinity of our origins, she does not say sadness or evil are gone from the horizon, no flies in the ointment or, as she has it, no devils in the milk and cheese. Persons carrying cheese appear at the sacred event of our holy birth. She no doubt derived this image from the Book of Job where we read: "Have you not poured me out as milk and curdled me like cheese? You have clothed me with skin and flesh, you have knit me together with bones and sinews." (Job 10.10f) Hildegard comments on how among the diverse persons who people the human race some are strong like thick cheese, and these children will bring forth "great brightness of spiritual and fleshly gifts" and will prosper. But others are made of thin and weak cheeses that curdle. These children will grow up to be foolish, lukewarm, useless. And still others are made up of decayed and bitter cheeses.

These will grow up to be deformed and oppressive people. Yet all three kinds of humans can be healed or saved.

Her meditation continues in a very Job-like fashion in the smaller scenes on the right which are to be read from the bottom up. Even though the foreground of her picture of our birth celebrates our original blessing, the background contains a hint of demonic forces or what she calls our "enemies." Life is not easy, she tells us. Our origins are beautiful but life is a fierce struggle. "Where am I, a stranger?" her soul asks. "In the shadow of death. And by which way do I go? In the way of error. And what consolation do I have? What strangers have." The soul wanders and struggles to "set up its tent," a symbol of our being wayfarers, homeless, spiritual voyagers. Setting up one's tent conjures up memories of the nomadic times of the Hebrews—the nomads and the patriarchs lived in tents, as did the kings during war. "To set up one's tent" also signified making a home. Wisdom is said to be searching for a place to set her tent or to make her home. Indeed, wisdom and home are often symbolically linked. The spiritual journey, Hildegard tells us, is a struggle to find wisdom in our home and in our daily life. Hildegard says that this Divine Tent came from heaven to each of us in our birth, but folded up. Our journey through life is a gradual unfolding and unfurling of this Divine Tent or Wisdom in our lives, whatever be the struggles and obstacles.

The soul knows what it wants but cannot get it— "I ought to have a tent by five square stones, decorated with the sun and with brighter stars. . . angelic glory ought to be in it. Topaz ought to be its foundation and all gems its structure, with its stairs made of crystal and its street spread with gold. I ought to be a companion of the angels, because I am the living breath which God sent into dry dirt. Whence I ought to know God and to understand him. But alas!"[8]

Was there ever a more poignant statement of the gap between our divine origins and the daily struggle on our way to divine destiny? Hildegard then recounts the obstacles, the enemies, that overcome us on our journey. Chains are put upon us, torture instruments suck our life-blood: "adders, scorpions, dragons and other serpents hiss "at us, a mountain and a river are erected by our enemies to prevent our crossing. Dante surely owes much to Hildegard here. And, finally, in the top picture, she is able to set up her tent that can resist her enemies. Notice that the fabric of the tent resembles the original divine gift given us at birth. At the deepest point of this despair, this struggle, this via negativa, Hildegard reports: "Terrified, I sent out the greatest shriek, saying: 'O mother, where are you? I would suffer pain more lightly if I had not felt the deep pleasure of your presence earlier. . .Where is your help now." I then heard the voice of my mother saying to me: 'O daughter, hurry for wings have been given to you for flying from the most powerful of all givers, to whom nothing is strong enough to resist. Therefore, fly quickly over all these opponents.' And comforted with much consolation, I took up these wings and flew quickly over all those poisonous and deadly things."

When her enemies attack the tent with their arrows she replies: "The worker who made this tent was wiser and stronger than you. So put down your arrows. . . . I finished many wars against you amidst much sorrow and labor when you wished to hand me over to death. Still, you are not able. . . . Go back, therefore, go back!" Still, the soul is confused in the tent and unable to accomplish all the green works that she wants to accomplish. "I send forth huge lamentations and I say: 'O God, you created me, did you not? Behold the vile world oppresses me.' " Like Job, she wonders why she was made at all. Where is her salvation to be found? First, it is interesting how it is her mother, the female side of God, that is called and comes to the soul's assistance in this story. Her pain includes the fact that spiritual joy has left her life and she can "rejoice neither in man nor in God." Remembering heals her; remembering goodness, divine origin, original blessing. "When I remember through a gift of God that I was created by God, then amid these trials I have a response to the temptations of the devil in this way: 'I will not yield.' " It is remembering the goodness of God that heals and makes her strong. "When anger wished to burn my tent, I depend upon the goodness of God whom anger never touched. So I will exist in the air that directs the dryness of the earth with its pleasures. I will have spiritual joy and the virtues will begin to show their greenness in me. And thus I know the goodness of God."[9] The goodness of God is not an abstraction. It brings about power and healing, delight and beauty. But it demands to be remembered.

Hildegard offers another meaning to the picture of the golden kite. It is not only about our first birth but also about our second birth, our renewed and regenerated life. She talks of the "New Adam" that we are to become by "hurling away the old one in us." She cites Ezekiel: "Throw away from you all your collusions in which you have walked crookedly and make a new heart and a new spirit for yourselves." (Ez 18.31) What is this new heart and new spirit? It is to return to "original wisdom."[10] We learn original blessing as we learn trust. We begin to trust in creation and in God and in that particular creation which is ourselves.

With newly found trust, our bodies can work for others. The goodness of God is our goodness also. "I say to you: Since God is good, why do you despise to know his goodness? For you have eyes for seeing, ears for hearing, a heart for reflecting, hands for working, feet for walking. Through all these gifts you are capable of lifting yourself up or casting yourself down, of being asleep or awake, of eating or of fasting. Thus God created you." Here Hildegard is calling us to responsibility. We can be strong, we can carry on the fight. "For when you oppose the devil like a strong warrior against his enemy, then God is delighted in your struggle." She tells us to let go of temptations to self-pity and masochism. "But you, o man, say: 'I am not able to do good works.' And I will respond: 'You are able.' And you reply: 'I do not agree.' And I respond: 'Learn to fight against yourself.' " All the pain that makes us what we are is itself power to be recycled. It is salvific. "One is able to be saved through the bitter price of pain."

Finally, Hildegard applies this vision, this holy birth and this dynamic struggle to set up a holy tent, to the Christ story. "The word through which all things were made. . .fell upon Israel when the same only-begotten of God came into the great greenness of the Virgin." He is the one who "pitched his tent among us." (Jn. 1.14) All that Hildegard has written about with this vision applies to Jesus and to us. To the Christ and to other Christs. For we share one humanity, one Divinity, and one story of birth and rebirth, of holy origins, holy destinies and holy struggle.

10. Adam's Fall

e saw in the previous vision the promise, the golden divine inheritance of every human. We also saw that while it is true every person is an original blessing, it is also true that evil choices and demonic powers and principalities haunt us as well. Thus, while the creation tradition does not begin its world view with original sin, neither does it deny a fall in the human psyche. In the present vision, Hildegard pictures that fall for us. Her story begins with the beauty of creation, the four elements that make it up pictured in the four corners—earth, air, fire, water. The stars are alive and shining and fiery and represent the angels: "Thereupon, I saw the greatest conceivable multitude of objects like living torches, having a great brightness. Those who took in the burning brightness received a very serene brilliance." This "great multitude of living torches...shine in a blessed life and appear in great grace and embellishment" because they "stood firmly in divine love."[1] But one angel, Lucifer, who was also a light-bearer and a burning torch, rebelled and sinned. What was Lucifer's sin? Essentially it was a sin of dualism, a pitting of himself against the Creator. Lucifer "supported those who wished to divide the integrity of the Divinity." Hildegard is following here the creation theology that the primal sin, the sin behind all sin, is dualism: the desire to separate, to make into either/or our relationship with God and the cosmos.

What happened to the rest of creation when this fall occurred? "All the elements of the world, which had previously been deeply calm and quiet, displayed horrible traumas and the greatest restlessness." Thus for Hildegard the fall is a cosmic tragedy, a cosmic happening. The whole universe is affected by sinful choices. (cf. Romans, Ch. 8)

What happened to Lucifer after the fall? He tumbled into a black lake "great in breadth and depth, having a mouth like the mouth of a well and emitting burning smoke with a great stench." In the lake was the "densest darkness" and, as we can see in her picture, the devil takes on the form of a serpent and the dark lake begins to resemble a certain tree. Hildegard, again protecting the reputation of serpents, says the reason the devil chose to be serpent-like was because "he knew it would be a greater thing to change himself into a serpent than into some other animal, and he wanted to take all precautions to totally deceive the human race." In other words, for Hildegard, the serpent is the *least* demonic of all creatures—this opinion once again places Hildegard in deep communion with the matrilinear religions in which the snake, a feminine goddess symbol, represents positive power.

But Hildegard's picture of shadow and darkly fingered lake/tree/snake, does not dominate her vision. We also see "a certain fair form of a man" living in a garden of delights. "Paradise is a place of pleasantness which blooms in the greenness of flowers and herbs and flooded with the pleasures of all aromas. Filled with the best smells, richly endowed in the joy of blessed souls, giving the strongest sap to the dry earth...that paradise is not darkened in the shade and in the destruction of sons,"[2] Humanity, "made in the image and likeness of God with such great glory and honor," was going to be tested. "Having been put together in heaven," humanity was to be tested through other creatures just as fire is tested through cold, health through sickness, light through darkness, paradise through punishment. The Creator was not stingy with the beauty and magnificence, with the original blessings that gave us birth. "Without boredom and with great zeal" the Creator made a garden, "filling it with every plant and set down in it the fruit of good trees and the usefulness, taste, odor, and good reputation of various aromas. This same lord, being a great thinker and a profound artisan, arranged in it every plant that could be called good or useful. He carefully considered how much protection he should surround it with so that no hostile force might scatter his plants. He also established his colorful things which know how to moisten the same garden and can collect its fruit and produce a variety of colors."

In the midst of this garden was a pair of lovers, Adam and Eve. "Perfect love" was in both Adam and Eve toward one another. Their bodies were at that "perfect age" as "when a tree begins to send forth flowers."[3] Adam was "burning so strongly with love for Eve" that he would do whatever she told him. Eve was a "tender person" with an innocent soul. Their love was a "pure love," one of mutuality. Theirs was a model relationship for others, for "neither husband or wife should cut themselves off from mutuality but should walk together in one will."[4] Hildegard pictures Eve in this vision as a shell with stars in it, attached to Adam's rib. We have seen her employ this symbol in Vision Eight above. Developing this symbol here, she calls humanity a "precious pearl."[5] A pearl is a hidden treasure, an obscure treasure hiding in a shell. In the Chinese tradition it symbolizes a "genius in obscurity."[6] So Hildegard sees in humanity a Divinity in disguise — stars, torches, and angelic powers are hidden and need to be refound.

Into this love relationship between Adam and Eve there stole the devil in the form of a serpent, "the old seducer." He was "angry at seeing Adam and Eve with youthful innocence so happy in the garden of delights." The devil, seeing Adam's love for Eve, conquered Adam by convincing Eve, for he knew that whatever Eve told Adam, Adam would do. It is interesting here how Hildegard does not put the blame for human fall onto Eve in any exclusive way. Hildegard compares Adam's fall to Lucifer's and finds it less severe. Lucifer "embraced the whole of evil and threw out all good" while Adam "desired evil and did it in his desiring" but also partook of the good. Adam's fall was not as deep as Lucifer's. Adam and Eve were expelled from the garden but God put a very bright light in it to disinfect it, to strengthen the place and to demonstrate that the "transgressions committed there should be destroyed mildly and mercifully some time in the future."

Hildegard subscribes to the thesis of "the happy fault," namely that Adam's fall made for even more beauty in the human race and in the coming of Christ. "Humanity shines more splendidly now than it did when it was first created in heaven." For now, humanity freed "shines in God and God in it,

humanity has a partnership in God, possessing of course the shining brightness which it previously held in heaven. This might not have happened if the same Son of God had not put on human flesh." Virtues abound now more than previously. "After the fall of man, more virtues were elevated and shining in heaven. . . . For when the land is tilled with much labor, it brings forth much fruit, as the human race has demonstrated. . . . O humans, look at that great glory that was prepared for you without blemish in the fullness of God's justice." For the faults of humans, Hildegard insists, cannot outdo the goodness of God. "The transgression of humans is unequal to the justice of God."[7] Humanity, Hildegard tells us, has been "elevated above the heavens, because God appeared in humanity and humanity in God through the Son of God." God's Son took the human who was tainted by the foul-smelling lake in which the devil resided, cleansed humanity of that filth like gold is cleansed in a furnace. "And he placed humanity back in its previous honor with even greater glory." So, humanity is even more blessed, more divine, more glorious than ever. If only we would act as beautiful as we are!

Once, when I was sharing this illumination with a friend, a Jungian therapist, he exclaimed: "This is the most mature person I have ever met!" I replied, "Why do you say that?" "Look with what frankness and honesty she deals with the shadow in her life and in our collective existence." Hildegard does indeed paint a scary shadow for humanity to ponder on in this picture. But she also paints a beautiful origin, a glorious future — provided we acknowledge the shadow together with the blessed origins and choose wisely which directions to journey. Hildegard does not become fixated on the fall of Adam, nor does she once mention "original sin" in this meditation on the Fall. In fact, later in this book, she talks about how some humans choose to "repeat the fall of Adam."[8] And, as we saw in Vision Nine, she celebrates our being born "in original wisdom" and as original blessings. God says to humankind, Hildegard declares, "I have led you together for great blessedness."[9] She is not advocating the excuse we hear so often that "original sin made me do it" or "original sin prevents me from doing it." Rather, her entire story is about how any and every human person is capable of falling into evil, yet being blessed with glory.

11. Recycling Lucifer's Fall Into Humanity's Glory

 n this vision Hildegard concentrates more fully on Lucifer's fall. At the top of the picture are the golden stars, the splendid "brightness that spreads itself out everywhere in its fullness, up into the heights of heaven and down into the depths of the abyss. There is no end to it." But one star, the brightest of all, whom we call Lucifer (light-bearer) leaves the multitude, taking other angels with him. "Lucifer the angel, who now is Satan, embellished in his beginning with great glory and clothed with much brightness and beauty, departed from the command of the omnipotent Father. And with him there went all the sparks of his group, shining in the brightness of life at that time. But now, they were extinguished in the darkness of fog."[1] Instead of "contemplating God in order to know him in goodness", these creatures wanted to compete with God by lifting themselves above him. Here Hildegard offers another example of dualism as the sin behind sin, for competition makes dualists of us all and robs us of any interest we have in enjoying the goodness of one another.

What became of these falling stars? "They were all extinguished and turned into the blackness of burnt wood." They were burned out and reduced to darkness because they failed "to be cognizant of good." What a strong lesson Hildegard gives us of being-with one's blessings, of gratitude, of being-with goodness, cherishing and being satisfied with it. Now these fallen stars, these burned-out torches, these darkened lights, want to make humanity fall as well. They render humans sinful by sapping them of goodness; they can thus turn humans into ashes as well. God tells them: "I will burn up in you all that dryness of the wretched ones." This dryness "will become in you eternal fire." For these fallen angels there will be no consolation of light, no wetness to extinguish the eternal fire of dryness and ashes. For humanity is "a temple in the building of God" and to lead humans astray is to render them dry and covered with demonic filth.

But brightness, not darkness, dominates this picture. Why? Hildegard teaches that the brightness once belonging to Lucifer has now been taken back by the Creator who "preserved it in his mystery. For the glory of that brightness ought not to be in vain,

61

so God preserved it for a higher light that was to be made." Who is that? Humanity. Humans are the heirs to the brightness and glory of Lucifer. "I the heavenly God preserved the bright light which withdrew from the devil because of his evil. I concealed this carefully within myself and I gave it to the mud of the earth whom I formed in my image and likeness." All fathers do this when a son dies, they keep that son's inheritance until another is born.[2] Since "the devil fell without an heir," humanity inherited his goodness. When humans fell they had an heir, however, and that is one more difference that Hildegard notes between Lucifer's fall and Adam's fall.

This vision, with its wonderful colors of silver and gold, its riverlike outpourings in blue and white, its green valleys and hills, celebrates even in the midst of Lucifer's dark fall, the overpowering grace and goodness of creation. Even at the bottom, the darkest spot, a sparkle is to be seen, hope is to be realized. Eckhart also teaches that even in hell the divine "spark of the soul" will never be extinguished.[3] Hildegard teaches that "no warmth ever goes to waste" in the universe.[4] One feels this kind of hope in experiencing the silver lights even in the darkest depths of this picture. Hildegard reinforces her theology of the "happy fault"—not only was Adam's fall in the long run a deeper blessing for humans but Lucifer's was also. Just as little David inherited the glory of the giant Goliath, she says, so humanity inherits the glory that was Lucifer's. God says: "I gave to Adam and his race the glory which was taken from the first angel. I do this because the pride of the devil has been destroyed and humans acknowledge me and serve my laws."[5] The original blessing that humanity is has now been renewed at three deeper levels: by Christ, by Adam, and by an inheritance from Lucifer.

Often when I have shown this illumination to groups, there has been a deep reaction. The idea of Lucifer's fall in itself does not provoke deep reactions in groups that I have observed. How, then, account for the response this vision provokes? I believe that it is in the primordial theme of recycling that this wonderful picture images so subtly. Lucifer's glory is here recycled into humanity's glory. The theme of recycling is a significant one in an ecological spirituality for our times.

12. Sin–Drying Up

The Holy Trinity, Hildegard says, is "a cutting sword that penetrates all things" and that "cuts always with wisdom and Power." In this vision the three vertical silver lines represent this "cutting edge of the sharpest sword."[1] Around the edges of the triple column triply cut through are, once again, the "fireballs" from Vision Nine. Symbols of the fiery spirit. The fireball is found inside water, which is pictured as green with its potential for greening power, and inside, blood (the top and bottom borders). Here another Trinity is celebrated by Hildegard, that of spirit, water, and blood. "Clearly these are in one and one in three. . . .They show the Trinity in unity and unity in Trinity."[2] The Holy Spirit poured over the apostles with fiery tongues and also hovered over the creation waters like a bird. It brings a "most burning greenness and strength" to all.[3]

The dark red in the middle columns represents the blood of Christ. By depicting the Trinity as a triple sword, Hildegard is contrasting what was a deeply maternal side to Divinity—egg, wisdom, quarternity—in Vision Nine with what is a heavily masculine side here. Iron and sword were associated with Mars, the god of war. The sword was often an object of much veneration among prehistoric peoples because of its capacity to ward off evil spirits. Cirlot tells us that when the sword appears with fire and flame it is a sign of purification and in alchemy, "it symbolizes purification." When associated with a tree, the two often symbolized metal and wood, war and peace. Among the German races, "it served as a symbol befitting high command" and was almost exclusively the prerogative of high dignitaries.[4]

What are the evil spirits that this sword is cutting through? What is it that is being purified by this triple, Trinitarian, sword? It is the sin of sins in Hildegard's theology, the sin of drying up. If wetness and fire are the work of the spirit, then dryness and coldness, which together make hardness of heart, are the work of the enemy. Hildegard writes: "If we surrender the green vitality of virtues and give ourselves over to the drought of our indolence so that we lack the sap of life and the greening power of good deeds, then the powers of our very soul will begin to fade and dry up."[5] This is sin; our drying up. Drying up destroys our creative powers, marking the end of all good works, the beginning of laziness and carelessness. The Holy Spirit, she tells us, sends "merciful dew" into the human heart to overcome dryness and bring about repentance.[6] But if we "lack an infusion of heavenly dew" we will be turned into dryness and our souls will "waste away."[7]

Injustice is the cause of sin because injustice is the ultimate dryness. "A person who lacks the verdancy of justice is dry, totally without tender goodness, totally without illuminating virtue,"[8] Hildegard tells us. A sinner is one who becomes "dry in the luke-warmness of his drooping soul."[9] Injustice is compared to "dust" upon which the Holy Spirit must send forth "rain."[10] The ultimate not-caring or care-lessness occurs when we become cold and hardened to injustice. For Hildegard justice is wet, injustice dry. Justice is the fruit of the spirit, injustice the death of the spirit. "It is justice which, when sprinkled by the dew of the Holy Spirit, ought to germinate good works through holiness."[11] Says Hildegard: "It is through water that the Holy Spirit overcomes all injustice, bringing to fulfillment all the Spirit's gifts.... With these gifts humankind might thrive in the moisture of justice and stream to spiritual things in the current of truth."[12] Salvation means justice for

Hildegard. "When the salvation of good and just people is progressing favorably, justice is active through the Holy Spirit so that such people rise up in victory to God and accomplish good deeds."[13]

Because sin is dry, it is subject to being cut open by the sword. That is what appears in the three columns next to the swords in Hildegard's vision. In the middle are pieces of dry straw, hay, or chaff. These represent dried up Christians who are scattered and cut down by "the most just Divinity of the Trinity." Cut off from the waters of faith, such believers are "just like hay which is trampled under foot and burned up in a fire. They have become separated from the fruitful grain which is faith with works in the knowledge of the scripture." Hildegard often urged church leaders—abbots and archbishops, priests and bishops, to stay wet and moist and green and juicy. She wrote one churchman: "When a person loses the freshness of God's power, he is transformed into the dryness of carelessness. He lacks the juice and greenness of good works and the energies of his heart are sapped away."[13] She writes Abbot Adam of Ebrach, "Pay careful attention lest with all the fluc-tuations of your thoughts the greening power which you have from God dries up in you."[14]

On the left column are feathers that the sword has cut in two. Here Hildegard is depicting people of Jewish faith who brag or who "trust in themselves according to their own self-assurance" or are people "of great pride." In the right hand column is wood decaying with dry rot. This symbolizes the dried-up faith of certain schismatics or infidels. Such people "are cut down on account of their rashness."

Hildegard critiques in this vision the distortion of three different faiths—Christianity, Judaism, and "infidels" or Moslems. But the sin in each is the same: drying up.

In contrast, salvation comes "through the water of rebirth."[15] A healed or saved or just people are "a fountain gushing from the water of life. Out of the gift of graces received from the Holy Spirit all their deeds will flow in abundant holiness." For these waters—that is, the believers—are a spring that can never be exhausted or run dry. No one will ever have too much of them. "These waters flow out of the East, and none of us can see their height or plumb their depth so long as we are in our bodies, because the waters through which we are reborn to life have been sprinkled by the Holy Spirit."[16] Christ is the one who made the entire earth to drip with heavenly sweetness."[17] He brings "to the believing ones the whiteness and beauty of life." Believers *remember* what Christ promised, namely a "water of regeneration" that becomes our "center." It is the foundation of baptism. The "water of salvation" that Christ brings provides "medicinal strength." People are not "whole in salvation as long as they are separated from this saving water." Water strengthens soul and body through spiritual rebirth.

It is interesting how Hildegard, in critiquing persons of three faiths—Christians, Jews, and Moslems—is hardest and longest in her criticism of the Christians. She does not criticize Jews or Moslems for their faith but for being dried up in their faith. Her picture holds much hope—for surrounding the dryness of chaff, feathers, and wood alike, there flow fully encompassing waters and blood with fireballs symbolizing spirit. We are capable of being wetted anew, she promises. For God says: "In the shaking out of my mantle you are drenched, watered, with thousands of drops of precious dew. Thus is humanity gifted."[18] No wonder, to be wise is to be wet. "The soul that is full of wisdom is saturated with the spray of a bubbling fountain—God himself."[19]

13. The Six Days of Creation Renewed

he viewer will recognize several symbols from previous visions coming together in this one. There is the darkness that dominates the center of the picture, which we saw in Visions Ten and Eleven about the falls of Adam and Lucifer. This "densest darkness" now spreads out into the world. It is the "power of death" and one can see it in the foul-smelling lake and the evil tree that Hildegard described earlier. At the top of the picture is a mandala very simliar in color and form to the Vision One, that of the compassion of the man in sapphire blue. In fact, this vision and that of "The Man in Sapphire Blue" appear back-to-back in Hildegard's *Scivias* book. Hildegard calls this mandala of fiery, cosmic ropes the "living fire" of the Creator God. "That brightest fire which you see stands for the omnipotent and living God."[1] In a later book, she would write about God: "I remain hidden in every kind of reality as a fiery power. Everything burns

because of me in such a way as our breath constantly moves us, like the wind-tossed flame in a fire. All of this lives in its essence, and there is no death in it. For I am life."[2] This divine fire is both "incomprehensible and inextinguishable"—it lives and no one can put it out. This fire has "never been blackened by any evil." It is "wholly alive" and vivifies all things. The picture also appears to be an eye, and Hildegard refers in this meditation to the creation happening in a "blink of an eye" by the Creator.[3] Cirlot tells us that the "divine eye" of the Egyptians denotes "He who feeds the sacred fire or the intelligence of man," namely, Osiris.[4]

This eye truly feeds the sacred fire of the human spirit— elsewhere Hildegard refers to it as "the living eye." She says: "In the living eye everything appeared in physical form." Hildegard calls the Holy Spirit "a fire that penetrates everything"; she calls God the Creator "a brightness that shines"; and she calls Christ the "flashing forth that radiates" divine fire.[5] Of course, her images of light and fire correspond to her image of a living eye, since an eye is not an eye without light.

In the middle circle Hildegard presents six smaller circles representing the six days of creation. Read these from left to right beginning at the top. The finger-like figure protruding into the six days of creation she describes as a whitening and "blazing lightening" which "stirs every creature up."[6] It has an obvious phallic form about it but elsewhere too Hildegard talks about "the finger of God which is the Holy Spirit."[7] The creative Spirit is like a finger stirring the waters of creation. Hildegard becomes ecstatic in describing the beauty of creation, its blessing and goodness—she has obviously meditated on the Genesis story where all creation is called "very good." The species of creatures "shine in their wonderful origin," they "glitter in the beauty of their fullness," and they glitter back and forth to one another. Indeed, "heaven and earth are resplendent in their abundant-making."[8]

If you look carefully just below the finger, you will see a lump of red clay with a human head emerging. This is the finger of God breathing life into the first human. "The same flame extended itself in fire and burning to a little clod of muddy earth lying on the ground. . . .The flame warmed it so that a body

and blood were produced. It poured heat into it by way of greening power and because the earth is the fleshy material of humans, it nourished the first person with its sap like a mother who nurses her sons. And the flame breathed on it so that a living person arose."[9]

Once again Hildegard celebrates both the dignity of the human and its interdependence with all creation when she exclaims: "A person contains the likeness of heaven and of earth in herself. . . .O human, you are complete in every creature. . ."[10] But she has an amazing point to make about the fall of Adam as depicted in this picture. When the Creator offered Adam the white flowers on the green plant to enjoy, Adam failed to do so completely. "He took in the smell with his nose, but he did not perceive the taste with his mouth. Nor did he touch it with his hands." This means to Hildegard that Adam did not take in enough pleasure to maintain himself—he did not allow the intimate embrace of goodness to enter his mouth completely, nor did he carry out the work of his hands to the fullest. Adam's failure was a failure to enjoy life deeply, a refusal to be involved with the goodness of creation, a failure in eros.

Adam was not sensual enough so he was not wise. Thus, "because he looked for God neither in faith nor in work," he fell "into the densest darkness from which he was not strong enough to raise himself up."[11] This picture story is most interesting for its naming of the first persons as red persons made of red clay (there is considerable evidence in these visions that Hildegard knew of the people of America and may have considered them a superior, or at least, more ancient people). She connects wisdom with tasting—*sapere, sapienta*, in Latin—and accuses Adam of not tasting deeply enough of the delight and wisdom of creation. She sees this and the reluctance to work with one's hands as the cause of the fall. A creative theological look at the Adam myth, indeed.

Adam is pictured, therefore, as being about to slip down into the darkness. But stars appear in the darkness and these, Hildegard instructs, represent Abraham, Isaac, and Jacob who are "great luminaries." The major and minor prophets are represented by the other stars. John the Baptist is pictured as a living flame beckoning the Christ figure

68

to arrive on the scene. Christ is pictured emerging from Mary's womb, the blue circle, at the bottom of the vision. A similar allusion was seen in the blue waters of Vision Eight. He is "driving back the darkness and shouldering it away with very great strength." He is the "new man"[12] who, emerging from the abyss and a struggle with dark forces, retains his complete relationship with the burning fire that is God the Creator. In fact, his golden color and the golden flame he bears make "gleam the holiness and goodness of the Father."[13] Who is this Savior who makes darkness retreat?" He is "the brightness of dawn," a "fully blessed man" who redeems people from "forgetfulness of the Creator." This understanding of redemption as reminding is very Jewish and Biblical. Eckhart also understands redemption this way.[14] Christ is the "fountain of living water" from whom a "great fountain overflows, so that every faithful throat tasting of him overcomes its thirst and dryness." The deceit of the lower worlds is overthrown, since, having conquered the devil, "he has freed his chosen ones from the lower world and by the touch of his redemption he has led them back to their inheritance which Adam had lost. When they arrived at their inheritance, tambourines and lutes and every song of musicians rang out in countless glory because the person who had been cast down into destruction was now lifted up in blessing. He set death free."

Who is this man? He belongs "inseparably to the same bright fire" as depicts the Father, for he is "the infinite Word in the Father long before the time of creatures came about. In the burning of love he was made incarnate in a wondrous manner. . . . Just as he was indivisible in the Father before taking flesh, so he remained inseparable from him after assuming humanity." While the "power of the Father is truly known by the different creatures of the world," it is through this perfect word of the Father that the Creator's goodness gleams.

So does Hildegard complete her story of salvation, or making whole again. Her gentle image of "the touch of Christ's redemption" stays with us. The cosmic struggle, the story in its universal implications, takes on rich and historical fervor. What is at stake is the holiness and destiny of creation. That is the Creator's concern, that is where the fiery light and the finger of God have extended themselves.

14. Sophia: Mother Wisdom, Mother Church

ne feels on meditating on this formidable figure of a woman something of what has been written about the symbol of earth-mother. She represents, we are told, "the house of depth, and the house of strength or of wisdom."[1] The same figure is presented elsewhere by Hildegard with a fishing net around her. In that picture, which is not reproduced in this book, Hildegard describes baptism into the mother church. Cirlot points out that symbolically a net is the weapon of those who fish in the waters of the unconscious. Ea, god of water and wisdom, did not fight the primordial monsters face to face but ensnared them by craft. The weapon of Marduk in his combat with Tiamat was again a net, a symbol of magic authority. . . .The symbolism here strikingly illustrates the idea that it is not possible for the individual, by his own efforts (nor, of course, by suicide), to escape from the universe.[2]

In both symbols, that of the stern mother and that of the net around the mother, wisdom is personified. Hildegard herself takes up the topic of suicide (that Cirlot refers to) in her commentary on this image, condemning it as the ultimate sin of separation and murder. "I established the body and soul together in the human person. Who is that one who dares to separate these things?. . .Wherefore the human person, who has both a body and a soul, since he is able to perform good work and when he is to repent strongly enough, let him not kill himself. Let him not fall back into that place where he can have neither work nor repentance."[3] The sea is also suggested in this picture by the "scales" (Hildegard's word) that adorn the bottom part of the figure. She reinforces the rich imagery of wisdom and water, of the sea and the *Magna Mater*. The scales of a fish,

Cirlot tells us, signify "protection and defense" as well as water and the nether world.[4] Perhaps one interpretation of Hildegard's image of church as mermaid with people in her arms is a kind of fishing symbolism. Fishing, says Cirlot, signifies "extracting the unconscious elements from deep-lying sources—the 'elusive treasure' of legend," or, in other words, wisdom. To fish for souls is quite simply a matter of knowing how to fish *in* the soul.[5] Given this understanding, Hildegard would be praising the church for its capacity to elicit deep, spiritual truth from persons.

Hildegard describes this vision in the following manner: "I saw a certain brightness white as snow and like transparent crystal lighting up the. . . image of a woman. She was shining with a reddish gleam like the dawn from her throat to her breasts. . . . And I heard a voice from heaven saying: 'This is the flowering on the celestial Sion, the mother and flower of roses and of lilies of the valley. O flowering, you will be betrothed to the son of the most powerful king. You will bear him the most celebrated offspring when you will be comforted in time.' "[6] In the center of her bosom a woman in red stands out and surrounding her is "a very great tumult of persons brighter than the sun, all decorated wonderfully with gold and jewels." There is joy and celebration, for "these are the daughters of Sion and with them are the lyres and musicians who play them and every type of music and the voice of perfect merriment and the joy of joys."

Hildegard sees in this vision how the church is like a moon. God says: "Consider the sun and the moon and the stars. I formed the sun so that it may give light in the day and the moon and the stars so that they would give light at night. The sun signifies my Son who went forth from my heart and lit up the world. . . .But the moon designates the church promised to my Son in a true and celestial promise. As the moon always waxes and wanes, but does not burn by itself unless it is kindled by the light of the sun, so also the church is in a journey of motion. Her children often make progress in an increase of virtues and they often fail in a diversity of ways."

In the two visions which preceded this one and which are not reproduced in this book, Hildegard discoursed on baptism and confirmation. In this vision she discourses on Holy Orders—but not in the restricted sense of ordination that we have recently been accustomed to hear in our theologies of holy orders. Rather, she treats the three "orders" of the church as she recognizes them in her day, and she has some amazing things to teach us about them. For if the sun is Christ and the moon is mother church, then the stars, "spreading out from themselves in the transluscence of their glittering, signify the people of the diverse order of ecclesiastical religion."

The three orders Hildegard celebrates are as follows. First the apostles, symbolized by the right light around the head of the womanly figure. The first apostles made this woman known by "running to and fro through various lands, gathering workers who might strengthen the faith." They are imitated today by those who "pass through the streets and farms and cities and other places of the regions and the lands to proclaim the divine law to the people .and to dispense the food of life." Hildegard pointedly indicates what priests and successors of the apostles should and should not do. They should not succumb to boredom, jealousy, or dryness. They should not be "blind leaders of the blind" but should be involved in constantly reforming themselves. They should "walk through the way of justice."[7] For when they lack "the fervor of justice," no fruit happens. "The winds fly, and the noise of the winds resounds, but the roots do not flourish nor the seed produce anything."[8] Sterility instead of creativity happens to the church under these circumstances.

Hildegard also admonishes the clergy to work for a living though not to seek worldly advances by the work of their hands. This is an especially impor-

tant admonition because among the signs of corruption in the monastic orders of her day was an increase of ordained monks who wished to "live by the altar," that is, make their living on stipends from liturgical ceremonies.[9] She urges the clergy to avoid shouting like useless and dry dust, to put on a new man and be green with compunction and repentance. She calls the clergy to their role as prophets who bring justice to the people so that the people may live. "Neither angels nor priests nor prophets will conceal the justice of God. Rather, they are to bring it forth."[10] The priest who is useful to others is a prophet. Good leaders are to extend spiritual food to the people.

The second group that Hildegard celebrates is the "most noble branch of the heavenly Jerusalem," the virgins and especially the virgin martyrs. They are symbolized by the maiden in red who stands in the forefront of persons in the bosom of the church. These are the ones who "courageously overcame death and are most wondrously filled with the highest wisdom." They bring a chorus of wonderful singers and a brightness greater than the sun to the Creator of all things. They bring forth their song "in the newness of liberty" and their chorus "bursts forth in the praise of their Creator."[11] "They sing a "new song" as the Book of Revelations tells us: "And they were singing a new song before the throne and before the four animals and the elders." (Rev. 14.4) Bishops, priests, monks, and nuns are virginity's "children" and appear in the background behind her.

It is significant that Hildegard chooses to place these strong and wise virgins in the forefront of the church. Strong women, she is saying, are the wisest ones and the most courageous workers. Virginity is not celebrated as being holier than sexual experience, but for producing wise and courageous workers. It is a fruitful virginity that is celebrated here, one of independence from patriarchy's dark shadow. This was a familiar theme in celebrating virgins in the church from the fourth century[12] to the fourteenth.[13]

The third group Hildegard celebrates in the church's order is lay persons. These are signified by the "white cloud" that goes down the sides of the scales of the woman's body. These people, when they preserve the law of God, "adorn the church of God the most." This group includes "kings and dukes, leaders and rulers with their subjects, also certain wealthy ones and poor ones and needy ones" interacting with the rest of the people. These people "embellish the church greatly." And their love for one another in marriage brings forth "the fullness of germinating strength," sons and daughters who people the church and make it green, youthful, and alive.[14] It is wise for married couples to "live agreeably" and not cheat on each other or break their union of marriage foolishly. "For in the mystery of divine wisdom, God kindly arranged this union of male and female for the propagation of the human race. And because this union was established so lovingly by God, for that reason the foolish desire of man should not allow a separation." It is important to note that Hildegard does not teach that sexuality is only about reproduction. Rather, she celebrates sexuality as the union of two human beings. "What is important in Hildegard's view is that marriage is not seen as something meaningful only through a third party, a child. What is primary is the union of husband and wife."[15] Hildegard sees marriage as a great good—men and women need each other to bring themselves to fulfillment. She counts virginity as a sign of Christ's sufferings, for it is a denial of a great natural value, that of the fullness of human nature.

Hildegard sees these three orders or groups within the church "embracing in a wondrous manner, and consolidating the happy church in the profusion of bursting buds and in the diffusion of the blessed greenness." Just as God is one in three persons, so the church is "one church founded by the one who is the planter of all good things" in three groups or orders. The scales on the woman represent the various other groupings of orders and ranks within secular society. They work their goodness of ways and their celestial virtues by "faithfully fulfilling in divine love the legal precepts for which they were instituted."

As one might expect in meditating on this strong woman figure, wisdom plays a large role in Hildegard's commentary. She is continually contrasting the foolish with the wise in her text—what constitutes wise as opposed to foolish priests; wise as opposed to foolish virgins; wise as opposed to foolish lay persons; wise as opposed to foolish artisans. In doing this she is constantly though subtly drawing on the parables of Jesus about wisdom and foolishness. Those who offer the gift of their labor and lives to the church should heed the warning from God: "O human, when you offer your heart to me in this way, consider how you may perfect it wisely. For my eye sees most keenly what the will of human speaks to me."[16] Hildegard is to be praised for her sense of holistic interconnectivity of different callings within society and church. Her lengthy meditation culminates in a passage on wisdom. " 'The foolish one said in his heart: there is no God.' What is this? Through foolish talk, he who was void of wisdom and understanding denied God in his heart. . . . He who talks like this is a fool because he does not have the true wisdom by which God is known." Yet even sinners, if they know God's creative power, can be wise, and God "will hold them like her friend." For God is the one "who gives life to all things" and will bring about repentance in the sinful heart.[17]

The law the church preaches and must itself obey is the "law of the Samaritan who led the wounded man into the inn." It is the ultimate wisdom, compassion.[18] The gifts wisdom brings "are always new and simple and the older they become, the richer they are."[19] Meister Eckhart follows Hildegard in this regard when he says that the first gift of the spirit is newness itself.[20] Wisdom makes all things fruitful, but it cannot be seized or possessed or controlled. "I hold the green land in my power. I never handed it over to you, o human ones, did I, so that you might make it grow whatever you want? No, if you sow your seed in the land are you able to bring it forth in fruitfulness? Of course not. For you do not give the dew or send out the rain or measure out moisture and greenness, or the warmth of the burning sun." Wisdom is much bigger than humans. It is cosmic and divine. It invites humans to participate and contribute to cosmic compassion. And this is the work and the sign of a healthy and renewed church. One reason why the church is pictured as mother is that it is to be a home for creativity. The church says: "I must receive and give birth."[21] What is it the church is to give birth to? It is to birth the creativity of peoples, no matter what their social position. It is to empower persons to birth wisdom and compassion.

15. All Beings Celebrate Creation

ildegard writes that "all of creation is a symphony of joy and jubilation." In this beautiful mandala—which is in fact nine concentric circles, one might even say, nine mandalas—she draws us into the experience of the joy and jubilation that all creatures celebrate together. Hildegard chooses nine circles to correspond to the nine choirs of angels—angels, archangels, virtues, powers, principalities, dominations, thrones, cherubim and seraphim. But it is striking that only the outer two circles are winged and angelic—the other seven circles have human countenances. Indeed, even the outer two circles are less angelic than we would expect at first glance. She describes the outermost circle as having "faces of humans" and the second outer circle as having "faces of humans in which the image of the Son of Man also shines as in a mirror."[1] She describes these two outer circles as "two armies of heavenly spirits shining with great brightness." These groups surround five other "armies in the fashion of a crown." The first of these (the third circle from the outside) displays faces of humans shining brightly; the next circle pictures faces so bright that she could not look at them; the next appears "like white marble with burning torches above their heads"; another were carrying helmets on their heads; and the fifth groups were not humans at all but were "red as the dawn."

Each of these "armies" Hildegard calls a "crown." Cirlot explains the meaning of crown in alchemical literature. "Planetary spirits receive their crown—that is, their light—from the hands of their king—that is, the sun. The light they receive from him is not equal in intensity but graded, as it were, in hierarchies, corresponding to the grades of nobility ranging from the king down to the baron."[2] Carl Jung calls the reception of "the radiant crown" the symbol for attaining the highest goal in evolution—the crown of eternal life. Within the creation theological tradition, of course, a crown reminds us of the theology of royal personhood—how God who is King has called creation to be "crowned" with dignity and responsibility. In this way creation endures, justice is preserved, creativity insured. "You have made humans a little less than God, and you have crowned them with glory and honor," sings the Psalmist. (Ps. 8.6)

Two more armies arranged as a crown are described by Hildegard as constituting the inner circles. The first were "full of eyes and wings and in each eye a mirror appeared and in the mirror the face of a person appeared." And in the innermost group the figures "were burning as if they were a fire. They had many wings and were revealing as in a mirror all the distinguished orders of the church." What did Hildegard see these crowns, armies, planetary spirits doing? They were a chorus, a choir, singing, singing about the marvels that happen in the human heart. "All these armies were resounding with every kind of music. With amazing voices they were glorifying God magnificently for those miracles which God performs in blessed souls." They were all celebrating the divine gift of creation. Hildegard reports: "I heard a voice from heaven say to me: 'The all-powerful and ineffable God, who was before all ages but herself had no beginning nor will she cease to exist after the end of the ages—she it is who formed every creature in a marvelous way by her own will.' " Hildegard gifts us here with an unforgettable image of Dancing Sara's Circle.[3] In this rich mandala all of creation is represented as interdependent and celebrative. Angel and human commingle, intermix, interrelate. Some angels are created, Hildegard tells us, "that they may help in the needs of humans" and others so that God's mysteries may be communicated to humans. All these blessed rings of creatures are "rejoicing in the joy of salvation," they are "bringing forth the greatest joys in indescribable music through the works of those wonders of heavenly things that God brings about in his saints."[4] Moreover, they invite us to dance a "dance of exaltation." We can join this dance, however, if we "hurl away injustice" and choose to perform justice. Thus Hildegard is also offering us in this rich icon a picture of compassion. Compassion, which is essentially about interconnectivity, is pictured by way of the interconnection of angels and humans. Hildegard lets go in this vision of the distinction or dualism between angel and human. Compassion is about responding to the interconnectivity of creation by way of 1) celebration—all the "armies" form a common chorus together—and 2) justice-making.

Elsewhere, Hildegard underscores the interdependence that characterizes our universe when she writes: "God has arranged all things in the world in consideration of everything else."[5] And again, "everything that is in the heavens, on the earth, and under the earth, is penetrated with connectedness, is penetrated with relatedness."[6] No wonder angels and humans can join so readily in a common choir—what does this say about race, religion, culture? What does this say about learning to sing with others? Hildegard says that ecumenism is a law of the universe, a way of wisdom, a return to our origins.

In delineating meanings to each of the rings of creatures, Hildegard says the following: The outer two circles celebrate how "the body and soul of humans ought to be servants of God." The outermost circle celebrates "the beauty of rationality" for the wings on the figures symbolize the intellectual powers that emanate from God to humans. The next circle reveals the mysteries of God and the incarnation of God's Son, thus the body is symbolized there. The next five circles stand for the five senses which ought to be regulated by the body and soul, the outer two rings of human powers. The first of these five crowns represents the virtues which "fight strongly" and lead people "to much strength to a good end of much brightness and blessedness." The powers are the bright ones, so bright that no one can behold them. No weakness, not death nor sin, can "apprehend the serenity and beauty of the power of God . . . because the power of God is unfailing."

The principalities, with torches and made of marble, represent "those who by a gift of God exist as leaders of men and women in their time." They must learn to "put on the sincere strength of justice" and "persevere in the strength of fairness." The dominations tell us to imitate God and God's Son by fortifying ourselves "with a strong desire for good works." The red figures are the thrones—they do not resemble human forms at all because they are so immersed in the "very many mysteries of heavenly secrets which human weakness is not able to comprehend." They are the color and brilliance of the dawn because they represent the coming of the Holy Spirit over Mary, the mother of Jesus. The inner two rings depict, first the cherubim, which signify "the knowledge of God" with their eyes and mirrors and human faces in the mirrors. And the innermost circle of red figures, "burning like a fire," are the seraphim. They represent "all the distinguished orders of the church" and they "burn in the love of God and have the greatest desires for his vision." In them, "the secrets of God appear wondrously." The innermost circle, which would be the tenth circle, is empty—it is the full emptiness, the via negativa, the hole that represents the "path of Transcendence,"[7] the mirror which is fecund nothingness. It is all things and no thing. Full potentiality. The source of all creativity. The mystery of the not-yet-created, the center where beauty is born. The number ten traditionally symbolizes "the return to unity," and the beginning of new creation. It also indicates "the totality of the universe."[8]

It is interesting to see how much like human hands the wings of the angels are. Also, how faces are smiling within the wings. And how the innermost red circles appear Aztec in form. These figures closely resemble the creator god Quetzalcoatl from the Aztec paintings found in the *Mexican Codex Borgia*.[9] Truly, the entire cosmos is invited into this living mandala, this song. We are all marvels of creation, royal persons, called to "sing justice" back into creation.

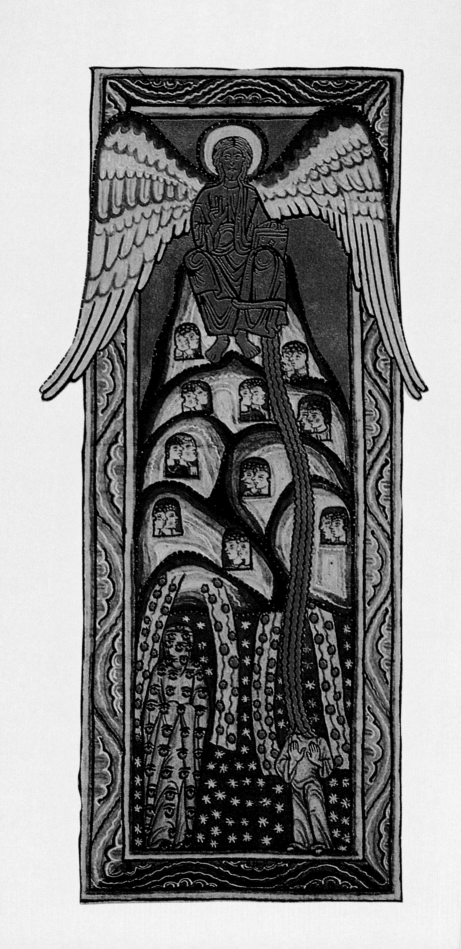

16. Emptying: The True Spirit of Poverty

n this vision Hildegard beholds "a great mountain, iron in color. Upon it was sitting a person of such very great brightness that my eyes had to back away from looking at him." His huge wings cast "a soft shadow" and at the foot of the mountain were two figures. One was full of eyes though without a face, and the other was a girl in white receiving into her the great brightness that descended from the figure at the top of the mountain. Many stars appeared on the mountain along with "pale white heads of human beings."[1]

Hildegard tells us that the iron mountain signifies "the strength and stability of the eternal Kingdom of God" and the wings indicate the "gentle and soft protection" with which divinity defends justice in the Kingdom of God. The figure full of eyes is the fear of the Lord "viewing the Kingdom of God with humility in the presence of God." It represents the awareness of God's justice that people know through their deepest insight into themselves. Cirlot points out that images of heterotopic eyes (eyes on different parts of the body) "are the spiritual equivalent of sight, that is, of clairvoyance."[2] Maybe we might better say, of insight. We have reflected somewhat on the spiritual symbolism of the eye in Vision Thirteen above. It is interesting to note how the eye for the Egyptians, who celebrated it as sacred, was understood to be the "sun in the mouth" or "the creative Word."[3] Hildegard elsewhere refers to Christ as "the one who gives eyes"[4] to people and she refers to the eye as an opening to the knowledge of God. Open eyes depict a good conscience, Hildegard says. Christ brings the eyes of faith, the understanding and knowledge of God. Opened eyes also come in the act of waking up, a theme we treated in Vision Two. Paul lost the scales from his eyes on his conversion. Seeing the face of God, the glory of God, or the Kingdom of God is implied in Biblical uses of eye imagery. For this reason we can say that Christ gives us eyes. Jung maintains that an eye symbolizes "the maternal bosom, and the pupil its 'child.' Thus the great solar god becomes a child again, seeking renovation at his mother's bosom" in Egyptian lore.[5] Yet there is another meaning to a figure with an excessive number of eyes. "In the first place, the eyes refer to night with its myriad stars, in the second place, paradoxically yet necessarily, the possessor of so many eyes is left in darkness," notes Cirlot.[6]

The girl in the vision "is clothed in a pale tunic with white covering her feet. These are the poor in spirit who follow after the fear of the Lord. . . . They do not seek to boast or inflate their spirits, but choose a simplicity and sobriety of mind." They imitate Christ, "following faithfully in the clear footsteps of the Son of God" since he, "even though he had heavenly riches, subjected himself humbly to the poor." Hildegard is describing here the theme of *kenosis*, of being emptied, of the via negativa. Christ, emptied of divinity, became human. (Phil. 2.6-11) So we, emptied of boasting and self-inflation, become divine. That is, we become poor in spirit and thus capable of receiving the Great Spirit, the golden and divine rays that radiate into us. We saw in the previous mandala how important the empty space is in the center of on-going creation. Here too Hildegard celebrates the emptying experience that a life of simplicity implies. "The one who rules all creation worthily pours the power and strength of his same blessedness" onto those who are emptied, i.e., those who are poor in spirit. This meditation on Christ's beatitude, "blessed are those who are poor in spirit," deserves to be studied along with Meister Eckhart's sermon on the same topic.[7] In both Hildegard and Eckhart we have a delineation of what it means to let go, to be emptied, and to be poor in spirit, and how important the via negativa is for developing receptivity to divine grace.

At the same time that Hildegard celebrates the spirit of poverty as the spirit of being emptied, she goes out of her way *not* to make a virtue of being poor. She points out, in commenting on the figures in the mountain, that the "zeal of human actions cannot be hidden or concealed from" God. Too often, she says, human actions are weak and lukewarm and emerge from people who are more asleep than awake. In this way people "make themselves weak and poor who do not wish to be busy about justice or about rubbing out injustice or about paying back their debts." Commitment to justice, she insists, would wake people from their sleep and would put zeal back into their lives and work. Poverty is not something to be glorified, though living a simple lifestyle and being open to emptying is essential. And so she depicts pairs of human faces on the mountain—one represents the sleeping person; the other represents the wakeful person who is "running the way of truth and is busy with the biggest works of salvation. He seizes the fountain of leaping glory in which he prepares the greatest divine things on earth and heaven." Hildegard celebrates holy work that we do on the mountain of salvation, the mountain of healing, celebration, justice-making, and compassion. She rebukes the laziness, timidity, and false fear of those who, in the name of a religiously pious poverty, do nothing in their lifetimes about justice and injustice. As I have indicated elsewhere,[8] the theme of spiritual maturity as wakefulness has been expressed in religious literature throughout the world. Hildegard is also making a connection here between wisdom as wakefulness and folly as sleepfulness. In the Gospel parable, the wise virgins stayed awake; the foolish fell asleep.

Hildegard's vision is centered around a mountain. The "Cosmic Mountain" is like the "Cosmic Tree" that we have seen in Vision Seven. It stands for the "Center of the World" as Mircea Eliade relates, the cosmic axis.[9] Myths abound on the journeys we must take to this cosmic mountain. Shamans climb a cosmic mountain on their journey to the center of the world. The Abakan Tartars as well as Chinese Zen Buddhists called the cosmic mountain "the iron mountain" (Hildegard, we recall, saw an iron mountain). In the Grail legend, contemporary with Hildegard, Monsalvat, the "mountain of salvation" or "health" is a "sacred island" and a "polar mountain." The polar mountain—and Hildegard saw whiteness on her mountain—is associated in particular with the theme of emptying, the Pole Star represents "the 'hole' through which all things temporal and spatial must pass in order to divest themselves of their worldly characteristics."[10] The summit of the cosmic mountain, Eliade tells us, "is not only the highest point of the earth; it is also the earth's navel, the point at which the Creation begins."[11] The sacred mountain is celebrated as Mount Tabor in the Bible, as Golgatha in the New Testament, as Mount St. Disibode in Hildegard's first monastery, and as Mount St. Rupert in the monastery she established. In her song to St. Disibode she sings: "You, o mountain heights, will never waver when God tests you."[12] The mountain is strength and defense, especially in a feudal society like Hildegard's. But it is also a cosmic center in the mystical and deeply spiritual cosmography that Hildegard teaches.

The voice that comes to her from this mountain is a strong one, especially considering that this vision is the first Hildegard presents in her book *Scivias* after her self portraits. Her themes of waking up, of seeking justice, of being emptied set the tone for her entire work. "And behold, that one who was sitting on top of the mountain was crying aloud, and with a very strong and sharp voice he said: 'O humankind, you are fragile like the dust of the earth and like the ashes of ashes. Cry out loud and speak about incorruption. . . . Some refuse to speak or proclaim this because they are lukewarm and dull when it comes to preserving God's justice. . . . But you— you stretch yourself in the fountain of abundance and come to light in the awareness of mysteries.' " Hildegard wants those on the mountain to spring into action. "By the flowing of your water, arouse" your enemies. "Cry aloud and say what is revealed to you with the strongest inspiration of divine help." God the Creator will bring "joy of an eternal vision of persisting justice" by way of our awakened and spiritual living and teaching.[13] Thus does the mountain heal. Thus do persons who reverence the cosmos heal.

17. Strengthening the Soul for the Journey

The journey to the center of the universe, to the holy mountain, to our origins where creation begins, and to our destiny is elaborated in this vision of Hildegard's. On our journey, Hildegard tells us, we feel like "a stranger away from home." The goal of the journey is the "crowning with the brightness of virtues."[1] (cf. Vision Fifteen above) In many respects the journey is a journey home, to our origins, where our Father waits for us—there are hints here of the story of the Prodigal Son or Daughter. This journey of setting up our tent (see Vision Nine) is a journey to the Kingdom/Queendom of God. "Therefore hear, o human, and do not wish to turn your back on entering the heavenly Jerusalem." To do so is to touch death, to deny God, to confess the devil. The Kingdom of God is opened up to those who hurry after it—but it is closed to those who remain content. One cannot make the spiritual journey without passion, Hildegard tells us. "O human, why are you living without a heart and without blood?" The choice to make the journey into the Kingdom of God is the opposite of choosing death or entering into death.

Hildegard's vision is about a double column or pillar behind a woman, the soul. Cirlot tells us that "in a cosmic sense, the two pillars or columns are symbolic of eternal stability, and the space between them is the entrance to eternity."[2] There is indeed a space between the columns in Hildegard's image, at the bottom near where the female figure is praying. The cosmic tree or world axis (see Vision Seven above) is also being celebrated here, for Hildegard makes the double column into a single one at the top. A single column also stands for "an upward impulse of self-affirmation."[3] Hildegard is indeed affirming the individual in this picture. She celebrates the making of choices, the taking of responsibility, the choosing of life and passion over death, laziness, sleepfulness. There is also phallic symbolism here, celebration of the female and male together, the phallic standing for "the perpetuation of life, of active power and of the propagation of cosmic forces."[4] The journey Hildegard is celebrating is no puny journey. Our lives are not trivial. They are great and demanding adventures, powerful challenges.

We are subjected to many trials in this life—"as long as a person lives in soul and body, many invisible trials disturb the soul of that person." We are called to "hurl away the deceits of the devil."[5] But many times "God hurls tempests on humans" and we who are "fragile in flesh" cry out: "I have such great and heavy things weighing my flesh down. I am not strong enough to overcome myself." What is needed on our part? Strength. It is the strength of the woman and soul depicted in this vision that Hildegard calls us to. "When you oppose the devil like a strong warrior opposes his enemy, then God is delighted with your struggle and wishes you to call upon him constantly in all hours in your distress." In the picture there are many "storms" and enemies that are hostile to the woman, who wish "to hurl her down. But they are not strong enough." That soul "resists strongly" and guards itself with heavenly inspiration. We are to be like her, grounded in strength. "Become strong, therefore, and be comforted because this is necessary for you."

Where do we derive our strength for this journey? Where does this "heavenly inspira-tion" that nourishes us come from? Ultimately, from the cosmos itself. For just as Cirlot tells us that the column represents the cosmic axis and cosmic tree, Hildegard herself talks in her meditation on this vision' of the soul as a tree. "The soul is in the body," she says, "just as sap is in a tree. . . for the soul passes through the body just like sap through a tree." How does this happen? It is a cosmic process. "Through the sap the tree becomes green and produces flowers and then fruit. How does the fruit come to maturity? By the mildness of the air. How does this happen? The sun warms the air, the rains water it." In the same manner a person's soul develops and becomes strong. "The compassion of the grace of God will make a person bright as the sun. The breath of the Holy Spirit will water him or her just like the rain. And discretion will lead the person like the mild air to the maturity of good fruits" or good works.

When this happens, and our soul develops in strength and vigor, then "the body of a person is made solid and is sustained by the soul." Just as the body takes delight in good food, so the soul takes delight in good work. The relationship of soul and body is one of mutual sustenance and mutual strength-building. "The soul is a teacher, the body a maid-servant. How? The soul rules the whole body in making it alive. But the body receives the regulation of the soul's work in making it come alive." The image of "sap" fits well the image of wetness she endorses on many occasions. What the soul accomplishes "in its body with its body" pleases God who welcomes us to the Kingdom of God.

Cirlot tells us that the pillar can also symbolize the spinal column of a person.[6] It is interesting in this regard that Hildegard talks at some length here about our powers of sensation. "The body is a vessel of the soul" and the soul is a "treasure" we come to know in this vessel. A person "sees with eyes, hears with ears, opens her mouth for speaking, touches gently with hands, walks with feet and thus sensation is in humans like precious stones and precious treasures that exist in a vessel."[7]

Still, how do we remain in touch with the sap, the wetness, the roots that will nourish us and sustain us during struggle and trial? Hildegard's advice is to remember good and evil. And to take the responsibility for making choices. For "through faith you know there is one God in divinity and in humanity." It is remembering the goodness of God, the goodness of our origins, our original blessing, that will give us strength. "God is good. God will accomplish all good things in me. When it is pleasing to him, he will be able to make me good."[8] To remember is to "look back to the oil of compassion" from which we spring. Compassion, our origin, is itself wet and sap-like in this image of compassion as "oil."[9] Hildegard derives strength from our "return to our origins," compassionate origins. As Eckhart said: "The first outburst of everything God does is always compassion."[10] When we remember goodness we recognize evil more clearly and we are ready to make choices. "But you, o human, when you remember good and evil, find yourself placed where two roads meet."[11] Choices follow.

How often Hildegard speaks of the strength of St. Ursula and her friends, raped and martyred for their faith. Hildegard wrote thirteen poems and songs about her, celebrating her strong soul, her cosmic beauty. "The devil possessed their bodies and they slaughtered those maidens in all their noble grace. And all the elements heard those piercing cries and before God's throne they cried out: 'Alas! The red blood of the innocent lamb is shed on her wedding day!' Let all the heavens hear, and in consummate music praise the holy lamb, for in this rope of pearls made of the word of God the throat of the ancient serpent lies strangled. Redness of blood which flowed from that high place touched by God, you are the bloom that winter's serpent storm can never harm."[12]

The cosmic pain of injustice is here redeemed. Indeed, Hildegard equates salvation with healing in this meditation.[13] We who have lived through the martyrdom of so many in our century—and the murder of four church women in El Salvador is one example—understand from a compassionate depth the deep meaning of what Hildegard symbolizes in the murder of Ursula and her companions. We are strong, a strong people who can make proud and strong decisions and take stands that usher in the news of the nearness of the Kingdom/Queendom of God. With this strength, a successful journey is assured.

18. Powers, Principalities, and Antichrist

editating on this vision of Hildegard, one is grateful for her advice on soul-strength and steadfastness from her previous illumination. This vision borrows heavily from the message, the form, the emotion of the Book of Apocalypse or the Book of Revelation. One feels the cosmic nature of human struggle because Hildegard does not hold back in her imaging of evil in human and cosmic affairs. She places the entire meditation in the context of our being in the "seventh number" or the last days, the End Times. Yet Hildegard does not settle for laying out a mystical cosmology—she also lays bare a sense of history and especially of moral responsibility for the direction history takes. In this regard she brings together the cosmic consciousness of mysticism with the prophetic consciousness of the Jewish prophets. In her commentary she avoids the literal conclusion of exact End Time—"no one except God will be able to

know the Day of Judgment," she declares. But she urges every person in every age to act as if the end times were here.

We who live in the cloud of nuclear destruction are no doubt more attuned to the reality of End Time than most generations of humans who preceded us. And therefore Hildegard speaks to us more deeply perhaps than to any other generation including her own.

In the upper left-hand corner of this vision we see five animals. Hildegard reports: "Thereupon I looked to the north. And behold five beasts were standing there—a fiery dog that was not burning; a lion that was reddish-brown; a pale horse; a black pig; and a grisly wolf." Each had a piece of rope in his mouth.[1] Since, as we have seen in earlier visions, the rope symbolizes the binding of the compassionate universe, we know that Hildegard shows these shadowy sides of humanity to signify the coming of chaos, the unraveling of cosmic order. What is bringing about this undoing of creation? She tells us that the fiery dog stands for humans who "bite at their own condition" and who do not burn with the justice of God. The reddish lion stands for "warlike men" who wage wars without considering God's judgment. The pale horse stands for those who put luxury living and their own selfish pleasure before the performance of worthwhile acts. The black pig stands for rulers who create sadness and uncleanness in themselves and their subjects. The wolf stands for those who rob others. The black rope, she tells us, represents "the darkness that stretches out many injustices."

In the upper right-hand corner in the East sits a "youth clothed in a purple tunic. I had seen this youth before on the corner of the junction between a bright stone wall and a building." This youth, now "shining like the dawn," holds a lyre in one hand and has two fingers of the other hand raised. This wall is a symbol of protection—a fact more than merely symbolic in Hildegard's feudal times—and a symbol of strength. The youth, says Hildegard, is the "Son of Man who is the beginning of justice who watches over the strength of the union of speculative knowledge and human work." The wall, being of stone, reinforces the symbolism of unity and strength[2] but also brings to mind the Biblical promise that

"this stone which I have set for a pillar shall be God's House." (Gen. 27.22) And in the New Testament, "Thou are Peter and upon this rock I will build my church." (Mt. 16.18) And again, Christ as the rejected cornerstone that has been elevated. (Ps. 118.22f) (We will discuss these symbols of walls and Christ as cornerstone in fuller detail in Vision Twenty-Two below.) Hildegard celebrates this Christ-figure as "the bridegroom of the church" who is shining splendidly because he "reveals the shining of justice in the righteousness of those who worship him devotedly."

In the bottom-left hand corner we see the familiar form of the woman who is mother church (see Vision Fourteen above). But instead of the scales that previously characterized her lower figure, a horrible picture emerges. "A monstrous and very black head appeared, having fiery eyes and ears like the ears of an ass and nostrils and mouth like the nostrils and mouth of a lion, crunching with a great jaw and cutting horribly like horrible iron teeth." What does Hildegard take this awful picture to mean? That the church will be attacked—but not destroyed. "Faith in the institution of the church will be doubted" and the "son of destruction" will inspire five temporal kingdoms to rage fierce battles among themselves." In the right of the picture, an ugly head breaks loose from the mother figure and is topped with human dung. Moving with "monstrous ugliness, it spreads a foul stench on the mountain" and "tears the institution of the church to pieces with the crudest greediness." It causes bloody wounds on the thighs of the mother figure. Who is this figure?

It is "the antichrist, the son of injustice, the cursed one of the cursed ones."[3] With it death rushes into the church. This can happen "because faith staggers in people and the Gospel limps in some people... The divine Scriptures have been rendered lukewarm." Hildegard addresses the monster: O you cave of injustice... your works seek the pit of hell. You will lie absorbed in your gluttony there and that hellish place will vomit forth stink. The world will recognize in this stench the bitterness of death in the destroyer of destructions." This "worst of beasts" joins up with kings, dukes, leaders, and those with money and prestige. He steals lands, destroys insight, and covers up the powers of the inner person to see truth. This "devil has no power in good things, but only in evil things of eternal death."

It is difficult to read these powerful images and to look at them, and especially at that phallic representation of the antichrist in the midst of mother church and not feel that Hildegard has captured some ultimate archetypes for naming the sins of patriarchy in society and church: its love of war and war expenditures; its dualisms; its sadomasochism and mentalties that do not result in joy for anyone, but in death for everyone; its dominance of powerful institutions of the West, including banking, politics, military, church, education. Hildegard furnishes rich imagery of moral outrage at the injustices of social and personal structures which unravel the web of the cosmos. For this is what happens when injustice is ignored: creation is undone, the demonic powers haunt history unchecked. "When the weak and the orphaned are deprived of justice," the psalmist warns, "all the foundations of the earth are shaken." (Ps. 82.3-5)[4]

But Hildegard does not leave us in a state of despair and defeat. Two witnesses are to rise up, Enoch and Elijah, who will lead the people back from Satan. These are symbolized, Hildegard instructs us, by the two raised fingers of the man on the wall. Elijah's return was understood as a necessary prelude to deliverance and restoration of Israel in Biblical thinking. (Mal. 3.4f.) He is a symbol of the prophets. In Christian symbolism, Elijah stands for John the Baptist, a prophetic precursor of Christ. Christ says, "I tell you that Elijah has come already and they did not recognize him but treated him as they pleased; and the Son of Man will suffer similarly at their hands." (Mt. 17.9-13) Hildegard comments that these prophets will "carry the banner of the justice of God" and stabilize believers in their faith and put the devil to flight.[5] When that happens, the woman who is the church and the bride of Christ "will reflect a brightness greater than that of the sun. . . . She will demonstrate a beauty that surpasses all earthly beauty." The demonic forces will yield to Christ, "a very strong warrior" whose powers will rise up again on the appearance of Enoch and Elijah. He will "break the head of injustice" which will roll away and justice and beauty will triumph.[6] Thus ends Hildegard's meditation on the lurking powers and principalities that compromise church and society.

19. The Crucifixion and The Mass: Cosmic Events

t is noteworthy that among the fifty pictures Hildegard has left us in her books, there is not an isolated one of the crucifixion of Christ. Only four picture the crucifixion at all. By far the most prominent exposition of the cross is in the present vision. How different this theology is from that of later medieval iconography where the crucifixion became an isolated icon in itself. It is evident from the present vision and from Hildegard's commentary on it that, far from being preoccupied with the cross, she sees it in the context of a deep and rich theology of church, of worship, and other mysteries of Christ's life. Hildegard recognizes here a tension of time—the already/not-yet tension. A tension of realized (already) eschatology and unrealized (not yet) eschatology. In the previous vision she stressed the unrealized eschatology—the justice and prophetic outrage that must dethrone the demonic and usher in a new age. In this vision she concentrates on what has already been accomplished to sustain us in the struggle for this new age. Much of Hildegard's meditations on this vision constitute a commentary on the Mass, which Hildegard sees as a cosmic event that "cheers the inner strength" of persons and sustains them.

Essentially what we see in this illumination are two pictures, one on top and one underneath.

The one on top includes the crucified Christ with the mother church whom we have seen in previous visions. Hildegard is celebrating the "happy betrothal" of Christ and Church. "I heard a voice from heaven saying: 'Son, let this woman be a bride to you in the restoration of my people. Let her be a mother for these people, regenerating souls through the salvation of spirit and water.' "[1] The "dark-red blood" and the blood mixed with water that flow from Christ's side fill the woman's cup. This is her dowry, Hildegard tells us frequently in this passage. "When blood springs forth from the wounded side of my Son, the salvation of souls immediately springs up. That glory with which the devil was cast out with his followers was thus given to human beings."

Who is this mother, this woman, this bride called the church? It is people, the faithful ones who are inheritors of the "glory" of Christ. The "only-begotten of God devoted his body and blood with most distinguished glory to his faithful who are both the church and the sons and daughters of the church so that they may have life in the celestial city through him." The gold that dominates this vision in both its upper and lower images celebrates this dowry of divine glory that the children of God are heir to. (cf. Rom. 8) "O you faithful people, you are the seed of the church. . . .You are not sons of the devil but heirs of the celestial kingdom."[2]

But the vast portion of Hildegard's meditation is not on the upper figure but the lower one. In that figure the cosmic event of the crucifixion of Christ is played out in human history by way of memory— there are four "mirrors" reminding us of the mysteries of Christ's life—and of worship. We know how cosmic the Christ event is to Hildegard because she calls the cross "the tree of the cross," thus reminding us of the cosmic tree of life in Vision Seven. It symbolizes the center of the world and the cosmic axis. She sees the cross as a cosmic event when she says that when Jesus Christ was killed, "the elements trembled."[3] She identifies the golden light as the light from "the creator of all things" who speaks: "I am the unfailing light. I radiate with my holiness the place of sanctification for the honor of the body and blood of my Only-Begotten."[4] Just as in Vision Sixteen above, a golden tail flowed into the emptied person, so here a similar golden tail flows from the cross into the empty chalice. Or might one say "grail"? The grail legend was alive and well in Hildegard's time. The grail, according to Cirlot, stands for "the source of illumination" and "above all, the quest for the mystic Center."[5] The altar is carefully lined up with the axis of the cross: it represents the new center of the universe. The Jews believed that the Temple was the center of the universe, and Native Americans still believe that the center of their worshipping circle represents the center of the universe. For Hildegard too, worship is a cosmic event. Power emanates to and from the center of the universe. Hildegard tells us how Christ, when he "killed death and shattered hell," actually "turned the circle of the earth in a different and better and newer way."[6] Thus this worship event related in Hildegard's mind to Vision Five as well, to the centering of the cosmic wheel and the renewal of the cosmos.

Needless to say, Hildegard sees much happening around this altar. "Suddenly I saw a great clarity of light coming from heaven with a retinue of angels. The light flashed around the entire altar and remained there until the completion of the sacrament and the priest withdrew from the altar." The same thing happened when the "Gospel of peace" was read and when the "Holy, holy, holy" was being sung. "Suddenly a flaming glittering of ineffable brightness descended from the opened heaven of the offering. It flooded the cup with its brightness like the sun

illumines that thing which it pierces with its rays. And while it radiated it in this way, it bore it upwards invisibly to the secrets of heaven. And then it sent it back downwards again, just as a person draws her breath inwards and then sends it outward. And thus it rendered the offering into true body and true blood, even though it appeared in the sight of humans as mere bread and wine." This body and blood of Christ is in fact the "dowry" of the church.

What does the Eucharistic meal mean for Hildegard? The "Gospel of peace" is to be read and preaching is to take place out of a "simplicity of heart" and not with vain platitudes and proud erudition. But still the essence of the Eucharist is to eat and to drink. For this worship is a "true and health-filled meal" and a dinner and a remembrance feast.[7] This is the meal we eat "until the newest man comes at the end of the world"—it sustains us on our journey of intense struggle as depicted in the previous vision of the negative powers and principalities.

"You who wish to follow me humbly with burning love, take this example which I leave behind for you, clearly my passion and my works . . . and faithfully eat this which I give to you. For it is my body." Why do we do this? "Eat my body because you ought to imitate my works in your spirit and in your body." And Christ also says: "Drink trustfully from this saving cup all you who desire to follow me faithfully. . . . As I gave my blood on the cross for the freeing of the human race, so I hand it over now on the altar for humans. . . . You are in me and I am in you."[8] Hildegard comments that people are "to be made cheerful through this sacrament," for its purpose is to render people joyful and merry. It is meant to "cheer the inner strength of people." The Eucharist "makes a face cheerful and this becomes the church with the oil of compassion poured over it because those who believe with the joy of faith embrace compassion. In this way they appear beautiful in the eyes of the Lord." Thus for Hildegard, as for Eckhart, compassion is half celebration and half justice-making. "What happens to another, whether it be a joy or a sorrow happens to you"—that is Eckhart's teaching on compassion and it follows after Hildegard's. The celebrative and joyful dimension of compassion is underscored by both mystic/prophets.[9]

In the Eucharist, Christ is the "health of life" who steeps us with a most healthy liberation" in the flowing of the divine food and drink. For we are made moist, wet, juicy by this "juice that springs from the sweetest and strongest fruit of the vine." Those who approach Christ the living vine and drink there "become green and fruitful from him so that they too bring forth the fruits of virtues just as he brought forth the most precious buds of holiness and justice." Christ "will never be drained dry" and neither will we if we stay close to the living vine. He is truly a "fountain of salvation," a "fountain of living water" who overcomes our dryness and quenches our thirst. He is "the living bread" who sustains us humans who so often "sink into weakness of our bodies."

Hildegard identifies the four circles or "mirrors" in this vision as images of the nativity (lower left-hand circle); the passion and burial; the resurrection; and the ascension of Christ. She compares this coming of God's Son at some length to the coming of divinity in the Eucharist. After discoursing on what makes a good priest instead of a "greedy wolf" in priest's clothing, she closes her meditation on cosmic worship with an appeal for compassionate works. "He who hurries to aid the poor ones is refreshed by the cosmic elements by the movement of his or her compassion. Such a person is greatly lovable to me, since he or she holds the innermost parts of compassion."[10] This compassion is greater than all other treasures, it lies in the heart of the universe and its elements. It constitutes the "imitation of God." It leads to action. Therefore, "relieve the lot of the poor," and "divide your goods with the poor." But Hildegard also admonishes those who receive not to do so out of greed or laziness or fear of physical labor. People should struggle to "be strong enough to support themselves" in both physical and spiritual works.[11]

In this way the cosmic celebration that the cross and the altar, mother church and her dowry gift of bread and wine represent truly makes the divine light shine in the hearts and places where humans dwell and where the Kingdom of God is to be found. This is reason to celebrate the cosmic mysteries continuously. Or, as Hildegard puts it elsewhere, "Let us be an alive, burning offering, on the altar of God."[12]

20. The Mystical Body Taming the Devil

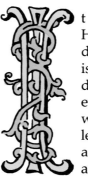t is evident from this picture that Hildegard, as we have already noted, does not repress the shadow side of existence. For all of her celebration of divine illumination, she never forgets evil. Here, Hildegard reports seeing a worm (*vermis*) "of unbelievable size and length" lying on its back. "It was horrible and mad, black and hairy, full of sores and pus and full of deadly poison. He had a nose and mouth like a snake, hands like a man, feet like a snake and a short and horrible tail."[1] Cirlot comments that mythic and fabulous animals that are combinations of species invariably symbolize "cosmic terror."[2] That is surely what Hildegard has in mind. There emanates from the beast's mouth a flame that goes into the four corners of the universe, a "very evil flame." He spreads his poisons, one of which is green, denoting "worldly sadness" and melancholy. Another is white signifying "tasteless irreverence"; another is red signifying "false glory"; another is yellow meaning "stinging withdrawal"; and another is black to signify "lukewarm imitation." All these "bring death to the souls of humans who go along with the devil." A series of "deadly plagues" haunts the world wherever this beast reigns unchecked. In his mouth are arrows which Hildegard calls "poisonous arrows of human pollution which people exercise according to their will against the law." Cirlot points out that symbolically arrows demonstrate "an undeniable phallic significance."[3] Is this another instance where Hildegard's unconscious is identifying the demonic with the patriarchal? We saw her use of a strong phallic symbol identifying the devil in Vision Eighteen.

But this devil, if we look closely, is by no means having his way. He is enchained and he is being sat on by a great multitude of persons who form one body with orange legs. "His head is trampled under foot, his left jawbone is broken." How did this come about? "Because his pride was destroyed by the incarnation of the Son of God." How is the devil being kept down? "I saw a burning light of great size—great and high like a mountain, with the top divided into many tongues. And in the presence of the light a multitude of people covered in white was standing. Before them there was shining like bright crystal a curtain."[4] These people were "trampling the same serpent strongly under foot and were sharply torturing him, yet they were unable to be struck by his flames or by his poison." The crystal curtain represents the law that always glows before these people. The mountain of burning light represents the light that burns in the faith of those who believe in the justice of God. It shows in the strength of its power the greatness of holiness and the height of glory and wondrously proclaims the various gifts of the Holy Spirit in the same glory." Still another time Hildegard is celebrating the royal personhood (the crown is a golden one) of the People of God. This picture of the mystical body triumphing over evil, then, relates to Vision Fifteen above where the "crowns" of creatures sing praises to creation. In a poem, Hildegard celebrates this same sense of a radiant circle of royal persons. "Good People, most royal greening verdancy, rooted in the sun, you shine with radiant light."[5] The parted flames, of course, recall the Pentecost event when the Spirit bestowed its gifts in abundance on the People of God. The multitude "shines in faith . . . through their good works." Their beauty and brightness enchains the evil serpent. "This happens because the faithful band of those believing ones . . . hastens to heavenly desires with much embellishment and decoration in the faith of baptism and with blessed virtues." They include virgins and martyrs and other cultivators of God. "Because they have been fortified with such great strength and firmness in God, they are strong enough to resist being befouled by the devil's attacks." For, "living justly, they grasp holiness."[6] Once again, as we have seen on several occasions, Hildegard praises the strength of those who fight the good fight. Hers is never a sentimental or passive spirituality.

On several occasions Hildegard has invoked mountain symbolism (for example, see Visions Sixteen and Nineteen above). But on this occasion she offers a unique comment on this holy and golden mountain, this center of the world and of the world axis. She says: "O you who desire your salvation so that you received baptism. Know that you are the anointed mountain of God. Reject Satan and do not wish to come down from the mountain of your salvation."[7] Here we have an amazing theology of the glory of the human race. Humans become other Christs, other centers of the universe, other anointed mountains of God. The Kingdom of Heaven is very, very near. It is already "among us." In fact, in a real sense it *is* us. We are the holy mountain. Hildegard considers it very important to meditate on how we are this holy mountain. Sinners are those who "have no happiness in God or in men." But good people overcome weakness and dryness by "attending to the celestial light" and are ruled by "good things and just thinking."[8]

There is an area of human endeavor that Hildegard considers to be particularly susceptible to the fires and poisons and plagues of the demonic one. That is the marketplace. In the marketplaces are sold "corruptible riches and vain glory, lust in transitory pleasures." In deceitful mockery [9] everything is for sale, everything can be consumed. "For the devil deceitfully offers his crafts to the people. And those who desire them, purchase them. How? If they are sellers, they relinquish their good conscience. If buyers, they 'consume the deadly wounds of their souls.' "[10] This warning about the potential evils of consumerism and the marketplace would be richly developed by Hildegard's theological descendant, Meister Eckhart, who developed an elaborate critique of what he would call the "merchant mentality."[11] Hildegard contrasts the consumers in the marketplace to those who "receive the wage of good working." The latter are the ones who are strong in their resistance to evil. Those people "do no business. For they, knowing God, carry the treasure of good will and the aroma of virtues and it is these things that they consume." It is the lukewarm ones who are easily victimized by promises of demonic consumerism.[12]

21. Five Virtues Building A Heavenly City In The House of Wisdom

n the previous vision, Hildegard showed us how the tongues of parted fire inspire those who carry on the fight to conquer the demonic. In this image she develops further the beauty of the person and the society in which the Spirit flows. Very little of the darkness and cosmic terror of the previous illumination is present in this scene. Rather, one feels the flood of golden splendor that glistens off the pavement of this holy place. First, Hildegard sees a "young man with a virile and noble countenance," very bright and alive, sitting on a throne. He speaks: "O, foolish people, you are lukewarm and are disgracefully withering away. You refuse to open even one eye to see what you might accomplish in the goodness of your spirit. . . .You refuse to be with a good conscience as if you lacked the understanding of good and evil. . . .Hear me, the Son of Man who is speaking to you: O people, remember what you were when you were an egg in the womb of your mother! Then you were ignorant and impotent to make your self into a living being. But at that time the spirit was given to you and with it movement and sensitivity so that you would be able to be moved and to live and, by moving yourself, you might know the fruit of a useful existence."[1] The spirit has given us gifts from the very first moment of our existence, gifts that allow us "to choose God in truth and justice" and to resist injustice and to make a contribution to society.

The first of these gifts is life itself. We must open both eyes, be awakened from our "sleep,"[2] to respond to these gifts. He or she who fails to wake up fails to realize that "you possess in yourself everything that is useful to yourself." We need to reach into our souls which are like a field and "root out the useless grasses, thorns and briars" to see the beauty that glistens in that soil. This takes work, we need to "work our soul and our thinking. . . .Do I ever give the fruitfulness of the earth without work? Neither do I accomplish for you, o humans, what I ask from you without sweat. For you are able to do work because you have everything in yourself from me. So, employ yourself diligently in work and you will have fruitfulness as a result." The earth does not produce without "the sweat of labor" but when it does produce it does so in "abundance and superabundance." The same is true for the work of the soul. "To those who voluntarily receive the seed of my word with a good heart, I superabundantly allot the great gifts of the Holy Spirit as in a good field." We are urged to cultivate our gifts.

Hildegard adds that "the best treasure your Creator gave you is of course a living intellect." This is our thanks for the wonderful gift of existence, of life, of intellect—to return the gifts by multiplying them and by using them. "At every hour of the day you should think about how you received so great a gift and how you have made it go to work for yourself and for others and how you might give it back in your works for justice. In doing so you are giving back the splendor of holiness because other people, called forth by your good example, might show forth honor and praise to God. Because when you multiply these gifts by using them in every way for justice, then praise and action of giving thanks will make God known. And it is God who breathed these virtues into you by the Holy Spirit in the first place."[3]

This Son of Man, dressed in red because he suffered pain and injustice, promises how wonderful human accomplishments can be. "What can you accomplish along with me? Clearly, the most brilliant of works. Works that are more brilliant than the splendor of the sun and are sweeter in inner taste than milk and honey. . . . For when you desire me with the innermost understanding of your soul, as you have been taught in baptism through faith, do I not make whole what you desire?" He promises to bring much to fruition in our being or soul and in our work. "I will plant roses and lilies and other very fine colorful virtues in that field. And I will water it with the inspiration of the Holy Spirit and I will root out evil from it by destroying uselessness. I am the flower of the field. . . . Supporting you, I will save you."[4] The work and the building that is referred to so often by Hildegard in this vision includes the personal work of soul-making, of self-understanding, of gratitude for life and gifts, that we have seen. We have been promised wisdom of a personal kind. "I will do everything which you desire to be done for you and I will place the house of my dwelling upon you."[5] Cirlot points out that the image of house corresponds to "the feminine aspect of the universe" and to "the repository of all wisdom." This house of wisdom represents "the different layers of the psyche."[6] We are promised in this image a centering, a coming-home experience, an awakening to why we exist and where we are going and where our center is.

But Hildegard is also calling us to a social task, a common effort at house-building, a community effort. He calls us to "faith watching and building in the city of God." How is this done? Hildegard explicitly rejects over-identifying this task with secular empire-building when she says, "the heavenly Jerusalem ought to be built spiritually without the work of physical hands through the work given from the Holy Spirit." The city she is speaking of "will be embellished by persons with the good works which are made by the touch of the Holy Spirit." The "holy stones" that constitute this city "are the holy souls in the sight of peace." They are those who "shine like gold." Why? "Because in good people wisdom shows its own work of splendor. . . . Good works come down from God into people and are moistened by the pouring over of the Holy Spirit. Thus the faithful person produces good and sweet fruit and obtains the company of the celestial city." Ultimately, the house that wisdom builds is the "church, which

is a mountain of strength. There I perform the work of justice and holiness," proclaims the man on the throne.[7] Hildegard is stressing how the "new city," will be made of renewed persons who are the "stones" of the city. Previously, as we have seen, she defined the church as people. It is not institutional success of ecclesial triumphalism which attracts Hildegard's notice, but the works of justice and holiness.

What is needed so that people can become this fruitful soil, these holy and strong stones, these builders of a holy city? What do people need in order that Christ may "perform the work of justice and holiness" in them as promised? The virtues are necessary and so the other five figures in Hildegard's illumination stand for five essential virtues. Dressed in silk, they are "cheerful." Constancy, the central figure, ensures that we persevere steadfastly in our good works by leading people to God through discipline. She honors personal strength and rejects cynics and wallowers in self-pity. "For I do not wish to be with the crying ones who are scattered into all directions when a wind tests them."[8] Two windows appear on her chest with a stag straddling them. The deer, Hildegard says, is the Son of God of whom the psalmist writes: "I thirst for you as a deer after running waters." Cirlot tells us the stag is linked symbolically with the Tree of Life and with regeneration since its antlers are renewed regularly.[9] We too are called by Constancy to continue running in our spiritual journey, no matter how great the sorrows or the obstacles. One is reminded here of Eckhart's statement: "One should run into peace, one should not begin in peace. . . . What is born of God seeks peace and runs into peace. Therefore Christ said: 'Vade in pace, run into peace.' The person who runs and runs, continually running into peace, is a heavenly person. The heavens are continually running and in their running they seek peace."[10]

The image to the right of Constancy represents Heavenly Desire. Desire inspires Constancy and keeps us on our journey. She too has her eyes on the stag and says: "I wish to leap over mountains and hills and the weakness of sweet but transitory life." She declares that having our hearts set on big and worthwhile desires insures that we will be satisfied, for "no one is able to be satisfied by abundance— you are only bored by it."[11]

The figure to the left of Constancy represents Compunction of the Heart. While of itself Compunction and sorrow and the lamenting of our exile can destroy the soul, with the help of Constancy, Compunction can hasten our journey "from death to life." She appeals to the hearts of men and women to "always hold to the true and eternal light" and not settle for falling into sad frustration by dwelling on remorsefulness and lamentations.

The figure in the lower right with wings had so bright a face that it could not be looked at. Signifying Harmony and Peace, it resists dualisms "and pants for the vision of perpetual peace." She travels to places "where all clear and bright things will last when they are cleansed from all the fog of injustice."[12] She too speaks. "God is just and one in sincere power and glory. I wish to embrace him always with a pure heart and a joyful face and to rejoice always in all his just works."[13] Peace and justice kiss in this image. They are inseparable in Hildegard's theology.

The figure on the lower left is a wheel with an image on it. The wheel represents "the flexible compassion of God." The wheel rolls continuously "because the compassion of God, bending itself to people with holy compassion and who are compassionate to their pain, is always flexible to those who seek it." The virtue holding a green branch in the midst of Compassion's circle is known as "Contempt of the World." This virtue rejects implicit values inherited uncritically from society. Compassion is not a value that society cherishes. The green branch that Contempt of the World holds in her hand is a sign that one must sometimes say "No" in order to bring youthfulness into the building of the heavenly city.

What are these five virtues doing? They are "trembling" because their time has come to be made manifest in persons, church, and society. They are ones who can "prepare the way of peace in the minds of men and women." They show "the beauty of the distinguished work of the blessed law" of God. They share the same image or face; each one "manifests God with equal devotion in the people who harmoniously manifest them in their works." These are the ones who dwell "in the home of wisdom." With constancy and desire, with compunction and harmony, with justice and compassion, we become builders of a heavenly city, a house of wisdom.

22. The Red Head of God Zealous for Erotic Justice

n the previous vision we heard Hildegard's invitation to build a heavenly city. This can be done with the Holy Spirit's work, human effort and strength of the virtues. In short, wisdom, which builds herself a home and which unites divine powers of the universe, can do the building through us. Every person whose soul has been "aroused for living" has wisdom.[1] The building of goodness is possible because we are grounded in divine goodness. In fact, "God is the one who performs in you what is good."[2] But confusion reigns. The church, which "ought to stand and be built in the celestial Jerusalem," is in practice very unlike the Kingdom of God. It is "imperfect in all its virtues."[3] Nevertheless, with Christ's help, the task of building this city is a joyful one. For Christ says: "Rejoice with me with praises and joy and build the living Jerusalem with living stones, for it was I who found humans after they had been lost through the deception of the devil."[4] The city Hildegard has in mind will have four corners and four walls securing it, for it will "collect many of the faithful ones from a cosmic gathering, a cosmic center."[5] Carl Jung believes that symbolically

speaking, a city with walls is a mother symbol. The city shelters its inhabitants like a woman shelters her children.[6]

The stones of Hildegard's city will be made of people who are grounded in the virtues. Its chief cornerstone is Christ.[7] Indeed, he has already "raised up the full and holy city Jerusalem with his every work and his hurrying back to heaven in the healing of souls." Hildegard is playing here with realized and unrealized eschatology, with the nuanced and important distinctions between what is and what is to be, between the Kingdom of God and the church. For Hildegard, the church is not the Kingdom of God. And the Kingdom of God is essentially people, not institutions. People are "living stones" of the structures of institutions, however, and she feels the way to make church more closely resemble the Kingdom of God is two-fold: human self-criticism and human works.

In the present vision she sees two walls coming together with a fiery red head on the corner where the walls join. She tells us that the walls, which are two of the four walls of the celestial building or the celestial city, are there for our strength and defense. They furnish "a fortification and a defense in good works." One wall is smooth and solid and very bright; the other is made up of stones. The first wall symbolizes speculative knowledge—it constitutes our foundation and our defense; the second wall symbolizes our works. (Cirlot points out that the walls of a city were believed to have "magic powers since they were the outward signs of dogma" in the history of symbolism.)[8] Hildegard says that the first wall "shines in the brightness of the light of day" and is called "speculative knowledge. . .because through it a person sees and judges his own actions." Speculative knowledge does not mean for Hildegard what it has come to mean in an era of rationalism for us—namely abstract and airy speculating, or as Webster's Dictionary puts it, "to review something idly or inconclusively." The word "speculative" in Hildegard's culture comes from the word for mirror, *"speculum."* Hildegard is celebrating our capacity to reflect, to look at ourselves, to be critical of oneself and of one's works. Indeed, the common word for this today is to be a radical, i.e., to question the roots of our choices. She writes: "This knowledge is speculative because it is like a mirror in so far as a person looks at his face in a mirror to see whether there might be any beauty or manliness in it. Thus, in speculative knowledge a person determines whether the work he accomplishes is for good or for evil and he does this by looking at himself." This, she believes, is what makes humans different from other species—our capacity for self-reflection and self-criticism.[9] The gift and practice of mirror knowledge is so important to Hildegard because "every single work in a person proceeds with this knowledge." Hildegard says that the ultimate reproach from the devil is: "You don't even know what you are."[10] Thus, the ultimate ignorance is ig- norance of self, a cover-up of mirror knowledge, a gross lack of self-reflection. This explains why, in the picture, one wall, that of mirror knowledge, touches the other wall, that of our works. Wisdom consists of good choices of action based on good motivations.

There is another instance of ourselves and all creatures as mirrors that Hildegard brings to our attention. It has to do with our being God's images. Mirror knowledge means seeing so deeply into things, oneself included, that God is seen to shine there. It is knowing how every creature is a Word of

God and a Mirror of God, reflecting Divinity and making Divinity shine. God calls creatures "mirrors" in the following passage from Hildegard: "I have created countless mirrors in which is reflected all the awesome variety of my originality which can never end. I have created these mirror images to har- monize in songs of praise."[11]

But where the two walls meet is a "zealous red head." The red head represents the "zeal of God" which is what urges us to wise actions. The zeal of God is essentially justice-making; it comes about when we are aroused by injustice. "In mirror knowledge and in human work there is a common boundary of injustice," Hildegard tells us[12]—person and society are wounded by the same weakness: injustice. Our actions for justice will not be just if we lack proper self-criticism. God cares so much for justice that in the past, under the "Old Law" of Abraham and Moses as well as in the present under the New Law of Christ, the divine zeal was always and continues to be for justice. "My zeal was avenging and avenges here my justice which was knowingly defiled in all the previously mentioned generations of humans. For God, who was then, is also now, and always will remain and my zeal, which was then, is also now, and always will remain, will endure right up to the time when the tribes and people come to an end. God's justice will not end but will shatter every rust of injustice."[13]

Hildegard describes this red head as having "a fiery color, shining red like a flame of fire. It had a terrifying face of a human person looking back with great anger to the north." It had three wings "of amazing breadth and length which were white as a shining cloud" and these wings grew larger as they beat and beat. The head itself did not speak and did not move. Christ, however, spoke. "This head signifies the zeal of the Lord who is the rod of freedom from unbending injustice."[14] Such zeal for justice is necessary because humans turn their backs on their rationality, their power for mirror knowledge or self-reflection, with the result that they become "hardened and deadened in the filth of injustice."

In the face of injustice, creation is not silent. The elements "cry out and complain loudly" about the evil choices of human beings who are rebellious to the wisdom of God and treat creation cruelly. "I heard a loud cry rise up from the elements of the world and they said: We cannot follow the natural course assigned to us by our Creator because human beings have thrown us into confusion with their evil works, just as though they were millstones around our necks.[15] Injustice derives from human forgetfulness of God and of the divine blessing and goodness inherent in every creature, including all humanity. We fall prey to this forgetfulness when we ignore mirror knowledge. "I am a work of God"—that is what a person, laboring with one's spirit, must struggle to believe, for it is in living out this truth that our moral actions derive their power. Very often, instead of meditating on our goodness, we choose to "plunder ourselves, to remove the good treasure from ourselves and replace it with wickedness."[16]

But all along God takes care that justice happens. Jacob was raised up "as the fitting lover of true justice" and all the patriarchs were instruments of justice. And Christ came, the true "sun of justice," and made justice the regular food for those who journey in faith. He became "the bread of his own members in the celestial Jerusalem."[17] Those who follow Christ are to be instruments of justice. Therefore, let people do works of justice in the joy of the Holy Spirit. Let them not waver in their perverse grumbling, let them not complain that they lack what is necessary." Let cynicism go, Hildegard urges! For, in the "fiery grace of the Holy Spirit," the zeal of God—one might say the erotic justice of God[18]—urges us on.

Erotic justice, zeal for justice, is an integral part of Hildegard's theology of wisdom. In this vision, she pictures wisdom as having three wings which allow it to fly around the wheel of the cosmos. In her poem to "The Virtue of Wisdom" Hildegard sings:

> O moving force of Wisdom, you encircle the wheel of
>   the cosmos,
> you encompass all that is, all that has life, in one
>   vast circle.
> You have three wings: One unfurls aloft in the
>   highest heights.
> The second is solicitous of the earth.
> Over, under and through all things whirls the third.
> Praise to you, O Wisdom, worthy of praise![19]

It is wisdom, then, and the zeal for justice that wisdom brings with it, that unites all beings in our curved universe. Cirlot tells us that traditionally wings have symbolized "spirituality, imagination, thought, intelligence; the light of the sun of justice that illuminates the minds of good people; progress in enlightenment or spiritual evolution."[20] Hildegard in her meditation on this vision and her reflections on "mirror knowledge" is also urging people to seek wisdom. For wisdom exists "wonderfully in the God-head's heart." So to find wisdom is to locate the heart of God. "This is the heart that sees the primordial eternity of every creature." To find wisdom is to return to our mysterious and everlasting origins. "When God gazes upon the countenance of humankind, the face that he formed, he contemplates this work in its totality, its totality in this human form."[21] To find wisdom is to see the whole of one's existence and all its interconnectivity with the whole of God's plan. It is to see what God sees—the divine image and likeness.

No wonder Hildegard says to keep touch with "mirror knowledge" if we and our works and our choices are to be wise and not foolish. We should remember in considering what the ancients implied by a "mirror" that their mirrors were often imperfect and gave back distorted images. Thus Paul speaks of our "seeing through a mirror darkly" or "dimly" and therefore seeing only part of the love of God that courses through our lives and history. (1 Cor. 13.12) But the mirror also conjures up for believers the "image and likeness of God" that we all are—"I am God's work" as Hildegard insists in this meditation. Paul develops that kind of mirror knowledge when he writes: "And we, with our unveiled faces reflecting like mirrors the glory of the Lord, all grow brighter and brighter as we are turned into the image that we reflect: This is the work of the Lord who is spirit." (2 Cor. 3.18) Hildegard surely holds this task up to us of "unveiling our faces" when she discourses on the need for self-knowledge and celebration of self as part of "speculative" or mirror knowledge.[22] She writes in one of her poems: "O, happy soul. . .you have been crowned with divine rationality which establishes you as a divine mirror."[23] The wisdom we derive from mirror knowledge becomes the foundation for our works of compassion and erotic, that is zealous, justice.

23. Redemption: Cosmic Healing, Cosmic Regeneration

 ust as Hildegard begins her theology with the cosmic ropes of compassion, the cosmic egg, the cosmic tree, and cosmic wheel (see Visions One, Four, Five, Six above), so she ends it in a cosmic setting. A cosmic judgment is depicted in the present vision. "Behold, all the elements and all the creatures were stirred up into a horrible frenzy: fire, air and water broke open and made the land move. Lightning flashed and claps of thunder boomed; mountains and forests collapsed. And everything that was mortal breathed out its life."[1] A cleansing, a healing, a purifying occurred in the earth and the inhabitants of the cosmos. "And all the elements shined again with the greatest clarity as if a very dark skin had been peeled off from them. Fire no longer held heat nor did air hold density. Nor did the waters rage or the land demonstrate frailty. The sun too, the moon and stars were shining with a reddish gleam just like the most splendid thing in the firmament. In much brightness and beauty they remained fixed and did not move around in a circle any longer. Nor did they make day or night to happen again. There was no night but only day."

It is within this context of a cosmic regeneration that humans too were awakened from sleep and from death. "And behold, all the bones of men and women wherever they had been buried and in whatever lands, were gathered together. In a single moment they received their own flesh, all rose up with their whole limbs in place, their whole bodies, and in their own sex. The good ones shined in brightness. The evil ones appeared in darkness. Thus the work of each person was seen openly in him or her." The beauty and brightness, the shining and glistening that characterize the renewal of the cosmos applies to humanity as well—but only to those who have demonstrated a likeness to the cosmos, who have cherished it and imitated its ways of harmony. These were "suddenly made brilliant beyond the brilliance of the sun." It is peoples' own good works that do the shining, the mirror reflection of their being images of the Sun of Justice. For their decisions and their activities in life reflected wisdom—their consciences were now unveiled for all to see. These "shine through the works of faith in the brightness of wisdom." What is the test of their wisdom? It is justice. "The works of faith are just." Like the elements which always seek harmony and justice, the human species too will be judged on justice and healed by justice. Indeed, the saved ones are the just ones—they are the ones "who did very many works of justice" even if imperfectly in their lifetimes.[2] They are the "builders of the heavenly Jerusalem who stand in the gates of the daughter Sion and will shine in the light of eternal life." Their perpetual shining will go on and on because it comes from "the Lord of all things" who, "with the brightness of his own divinity, gives them light."

Unlike the rest of creation, humanity can choose injustice instead of justice; folly instead of wisdom if it cares to. However, those who do will never be cleansed, healed, made one with the regenerated cosmos. They will be "the unjust ones who did evil works." They exist with a shadow before their faces in the lower right-hand corner of the picture in the company of their chained diabolic leader. They must live with the "darkness of their own neglect" because they extinguished works of justice and creativity in their lifetimes.

As the lower circle in the vision depicts the tumult in the elements of creation, so the upper circle shows the coming of the Son of Man who inaugurates this time of regeneration, or what Hildegard calls "the newest times" (*novissima tempora*). In these times time itself "will be changed into the eternity of that flashing One who is without end."[3] Christ appears from the East amidst a great flash. He has the same facial expression as he had in the world and his wounds are open. He speaks to the just and wise ones "with a caressing voice" and to the others "with a frightful voice." He alerts the cosmos to the truth about itself—to the just he reveals their justice; to the unjust their foolishness; and to the elements of the world their cleansing and harmonizing, for "every creature knows him to be the Son of God."

It is important that we not understand Hildegard's description of these "newest times" in an exclusively literal way as regards a Last Judgment of the world. Mircea Eliade points out that "the most representative mystical experience of the archaic societies [is] the desire to restore communication between Earth and Heaven." While Christianity offers three ways of doing this, first by way of baptism, and last by way of death, the mystical way is the deeper way. "It is mysticism that best exemplifies the restoration of the life of Paradise."[4] Mysticism, of course, happens in this life. And there is much in Hildegard's vision, especially when it is understood in the context of her complete thought, to emphasize the "now" aspect, the realized eschatology aspect, of this scene of cosmic regeneration. Cirlot offers a similar caution when he notes that the Day of Judgment, awakening the dead with trumpets and images of gold and sun symbolism, often signifies the awakening of the soul from death to life. "Death, in the symbolic sense, is equivalent to the death of the soul—to ignoring the transcendental aim of Man. . . . The angel, by means both of his light and of his trumpet-call, 'awakens' the latent desire for resurrection in the man who has fallen into iniquity."[5] I believe Hildegard would heartily concur in his emphasis on the "this-life" approach to a scene of judgment. After all, it is she who insists on several occasions on how important it is that our work be "useful."

This scene of judgment and regeneration can also be understood as a treatise on creativity or the *via creativa*. Hildegard paints a picture of the cosmic chaos and disturbance that immediately precedes the judgment, that is the decision making that every human—and the Christ in every human— must make as to what images one will follow and will give birth to in his or her life. The via negativa and the via creativa come together powerfully in this image of Hildegard's. She says: " A human, when his life is drawing to a close, is overtaken with many weaknesses. He is cast down so that at the hour of his death he is broken up with much sorrow. In the same way very great adversities will precede the end of the world and they will break it up at its end with diverse terrors. Consider that the elements too will display their terrors at that time."[6] Every artist and birther at every act of birth has tasted of the cosmic terror that precedes creativity. It is truly a "Last Judgment" in the sense that every creative act is a "last time occasion," that is to say a "one-and-only-time" occasion. One either births at this particular moment in history or one chooses not to birth. The particular moment will never repeat itself again and therefore it is a final moment, a Last Judgment. Hildegard's advice to the artist in us and among us is that there is no need to fear this crucial moment provided one's decision making has been based on justice and cosmic wisdom. This is one important way to understand the traditions of the Last Judgment and the Second Coming within the context of a realized eschatology.

One cannot meditate on this illumination of Hildegard's without feeling the overpowering presence of the color red. Hildegard says that a "reddish gleam" dominates the scene and indeed red does dominate. According to Jungian psychologist Jolan Jacobi, red symbolizes "pulsing blood and fire, the surging and tearing emotions." It is associated with "blood, wounds, death-throes and sublimation." It also indicates transition, being mid-way between yellow (white) and blue (black). Red is the color of Mars and denotes "passion, sentiment and the life-giving principle" according to Cirlot. It is also the color that represents the mother goddess of India and in alchemy, the three main phases of the "Great Work" culminate in red (sulphur) which in turn yields gold, the "state of glory."[7] No one could suggest that Hildegard's picture of justice and judgment, of regeneration of cosmos and human, lacks compassion. She concludes: "Let him or her who has keen ears of inner understanding pant for these words with a burning love for my image. And let her write these things in the conscience of her soul."[8]

24. New Heaven, New Earth

n this illumination, dominated not by red but by Hildegard's favorite color, green, we experience the peace and harmony that follows the winnowing out of injustice from the cosmos. After all, the elements themselves have suffered grievously from the injustice and callousness of human decisions. All the elements cry out when humans treat them unjustly and Hildegard teaches that when Cain killed Abel, the earth was torn asunder. "When Abel's blood was shed, the entire earth sighed and at that moment was declared a widow: Just as a woman without the comfort of her husband remains fixed in her widowhood, the earth was also robbed of its holy totality by the murder committed by Cain."[1] It is evident from the lessons from Hildegard's previous vision and from the experience of the present one that earth's long widowhood is ended. The "holy integrity" which characterizes creation has returned. The weeping will be heard no longer. Harmony and tranquility reign. This is how Hildegard describes the present image. "And so, with the judgment completed, the flashes of lightning and the claps of thunder and the winds and storms ceased. Whatever there was of changes in the elements vanished and a very great tranquility came about."[2] For "all things have been cleansed" and whatever was foul in the world vanishes "just like salt that dissolves when it is put into water." And now there arises "out of the divine plan the greatest quiet and tranquility." The Paradise Hildegard is describing is a kind of Sabbath, a day or age of Rest, a temporal Paradise where integrity is regained and peace, not dualism, reigns.

111

Every creature maintains its own form and expression and none is disturbed. Rest permeates everything—even the heavens cease to move. This is the deeper meaning of the Sabbath day for the Jewish people—not that it was just "a day off" but that it was a time that was "set aside for experiencing the spontaneous, perfect harmony of humans in Nature."[3] It was a time for wisdom to reign instead of business, competition, and struggle. In taking up the subject of repose, Hildegard is developing a very rich topic in wisdom literature. It brings together many of the themes of spiritual journeying, of setting up one's tent, building the holy city of Jerusalem, climbing the mountain, bearing green fruit. Consider this passage from the Book of Sirach. Wisdom is speaking.

> *Then the Creator of all things instructed me,*
> *he who created me fixed a place for my tent.*
> *He said, 'Pitch your tent in Jacob,*
> *make Israel your inheritance.'*
> *From eternity, in the beginning, he created me,*
> *and for eternity I shall remain.*
> *I ministered before him in the holy tabernacle,*
> *and thus was I established in Zion.*
> *In the beloved city he has given me rest,*
> *and in Jerusalem I wield my authority.*
> *I have taken root in a privileged people,*
> *in the Lord's property, in his inheritance . . .*
> *I am like a vine putting out graceful shoots,*
> *my blossoms bear the fruit of glory and wealth.*
>
> (Si. 24.6-12,17)

Meister Eckhart, in a sermon rightly named "How All Creatures Experience the Divine Repose," develops this same theme of the Sabbath of creation. He says that "the Creator seeks to draw all creatures with him back again to their origin, which is repose." The first, second, third, and fourth purpose of creation, he maintains, is "Repose."[4]

Hildegard celebrates this New Heaven and New Earth relationship in this picture of three rings. The lower ring contains the cosmic processes—flames of fire, flames of air, surround the ring of stars, sky, flowers, herbs and water. Thus the four elements, earth, air, fire, water, are all in place and at harmony, namely at rest. The middle ring contains the "builders of the city of Zion"—the "great celestial army" of the chosen ones who "possess the brightness of eternity and seek celestial joys in great glory." The gold of divine glory and light bathes them all. These include "the patriarchs and prophets who lived before Christ's incarnation, the apostles who talked with him in time, the martyrs, confessors, virgins, widows, who imitated him faithfully." It also includes church leaders and secular leaders, hermits and monarchs. All are enjoying "celestial joys."[5] The top ring pictures the Creator with the lamb of God, the Son of God, in his lap, both surrounded by the green ring of the Holy Spirit and basked in divine light depicted in gold. The Creator holds a fleur-de-lis as do some of the humans in the middle circle. The fleur-de-lis is a frequently used symbol in the Middle Ages for "illumination and as an attribute of the Lord."[6] Also, because it symbolizes royalty, Hildegard celebrates the royal personhood of all believers and their relationship to God, the Creator King.

It is significant in Hildegard's theology that of the three rings—Divinity, humanity and creation—humanity is placed in the center. "Divinity is aimed at humanity," she declares.[7] Humanity is meant to be a bridge, a link, a bonding force such as a marriage ring symbolizes between Divinity and nature. "Humanity finds itself in the middle of the world. In the middle of all other creatures humanity is the most significant and yet the most dependent on the others."[8] The green that so dominates the rings and the frame around the rings is Hildegard's promise of *viriditas*, greening power, moistness and quenching of thirst that wisdom herself promises. (See Vision Three above.) "Then let all who are thirsty come. All who want it may have the water of life, and have it free." (Rev. 21.17) Here, under the banner of Greening Power, the promise of the prophet Isaiah is fulfilled. "For now I create new heavens and a new earth, and the past will not be remembered, and will come no more to people's minds. . . .They will do no hurt, nor harm on all my holy mountain, says Yahweh." (Is. 65.17,15) This is what the author of the Book of Revelations, who figures so prominently in Visions Eighteen and Twenty-Three, reports: "Then I saw a new heaven and a new earth; the first heaven and the first earth had disappeared now, and there was no longer any sea. I saw the holy city and the new Jerusalem, coming down from God out of heaven as beautiful as a bride all dressed for her husband. . . .Then the One sitting on the throne spoke: 'Now I am making the whole of creation new,' he said. 'Write this: That what I am saying is sure and will come true.' And then he said, 'It is already done.' " (Rev. 21.1,2,5,6)

Indeed, it is already done. Greening power and rest have arrived. And the harmonious life that wisdom promises. And the Good News renders all things new.

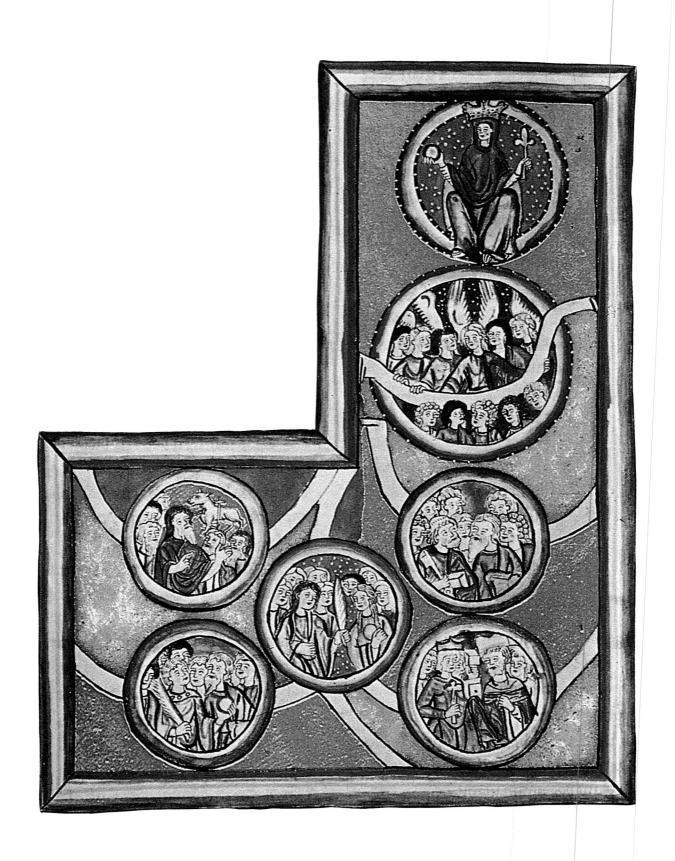

25. The Communion of Saints in Cosmic Symphony

n this, the final illumination in Hildegard's book, *Scivias*, Hildegard pictures the communion of saints in heaven. Who are the saints? Saints for Hildegard are those who take on the two dimensions of being human, namely to celebrate and to do works of justice. These usher compassion into history; these bring the "surprise of God" into the world. "Humankind demonstrates two aspects: the singing of praise to God, and the doing of good works. God is made known through praise, and in good works the wonders of God can be seen."[1] Who, then, are these saints? "Here were the blessed ones, the happy ones, who moved God in their time and stirred God with sincere striving and just works." What are they doing? They are enjoying themselves "with unbounded delight. . .with every manner of sweet blossoming, with every manner of good aromas and lovely scents. . . .Now in all this marvelousness they can enjoy the sweetest ecstasy."[2] But we dwellers on earth are also called to the Sabbath, to the Day of Rest, to delight and praise, to ecstasy, to network with the communion of saints. The Day of Rest that Hildegard celebrated in our previous illumination is not a day of doing nothing but a day of being, and celebrating being. And our doing it together. She says: "Be not lax in celebrating. Be not lazy in the festive service of God. Be ablaze with enthusiasm. Let us be an alive, burning offering before the altar of God!"[3]

For Hildegard, there is no truer, deeper, or more cosmic way to celebrate being than to make music. She writes: "Through the power of hearing, God opens to human beings all the glorious sounds of the hidden mysteries and of the choirs of angels by whom God is praised over and over again. It would be unfitting if God could not be recognized in the same manner that one person recognizes another, namely by his or her hearing powers. Indeed, here human beings from within their own selves, come to an understanding of the whole. We would be empty were we not able to hear and comprehend."[4] For Hildegard, cosmic celebration is inconceivable without hearing music—our "understanding of the whole" happens this way. It is our way to wisdom and our celebration of wisdom, for "wisdom resides in all works of art."[5] We will recall the title of her collection of seventy-seven songs which she composed and for which she wrote the words, "Symphony of the Harmony of the Heavenly Revelations." Cosmos and music go together for her—as do justice-making and peaceful or harmonious living.

In her meditation on the present vision, Hildegard lays the groundwork for an entire theology of music. For her, God is music. "O Trinity, you are music, you are life."[6] The gold that permeates the picture represents the divine life that permeates the cosmos like music itself. The gold is interlaced with blues. Together they paint for us "a very bright sky, standing for the joy of the celestial cities" in which wonderful music is heard. "A pleasant and fine symphony of sounds with the wondrous joys of the chosen ones" there. Mysteries are learned through this music that are learned no other way.[7] Music renders public the glory and honor of the heavenly cities—it gets the sound out into the universe. Word and music go together like body and spirit.

"The word stands for the body, but the symphony stands for the spirit." Music announces the divinity and word unveils the humanity of God's Son. Music is so valuable for our spiritual lives because it wakes us up. It "arouses sluggish souls to watchfulness." Prophets like King David in his psalms and Jeremiah in his lamentations resorted to music. Music has the power to soften "even hard hearts" and by rendering hearts moist it ushers in the Holy Spirit. It overcomes disagreements and divisions and creates harmony. "So too, you o men and women, who are poor and frail in nature, hear in music the sound from the fiery love of the virginal blush that flowers like a green twig in the embrace of words. Hear the sound from the peak of the living lights shining in the celestial city. Hear the sound from the prophecy of deep preaching. Hear the sound from the wonderful words of the missions of the apostles. Hear the sound from the office of the priestly mysteries."

What is music doing in all these instances? It is creation "rebounding to the celestial Creator with a single voice of exultation and joy and the giving of thanks." Music is the way to give gratitude to God. Music is not restricted to the two-legged ones. The whole universe makes music from its harmonious interconnectivity. "All of creation is a song of praise to God," Hildegard writes.

The fire has its flames and praises God.
The wind blows the flame and praises God.
In the voice we hear the word which praises God.
And the word, when heard, praises God.
So all of creation is a song of praise to God.[8]

While Hildegard declares that the human soul "is a symphony," she believes that creation itself is also. "All of creation is a symphony of the Holy Spirit which is joy and jubilation." The chorus of the communion of saints integrates itself into the greater chorus of the cosmos itself. Or, as Thomas Merton said, "every non two-legged creature is a saint."

In a letter written late in her life when her monastery was closed down by interdiction, she develops her profound theology of music based on her theology of prophecy and creation. She says that the prophets, needing to be "aroused to the praises of the Creator," composed psalms, wrote canticles, played these for their listeners, and also created various musical instruments. Those through the ages who invented other musical instruments were simply imitating the holy prophets. "The prophetic spirit," she declares, "orders that God be praised with cymbals of jubilation and with the rest of the musical instruments. . . ." Not only the prophets, but creation itself dictates that we celebrate with music. Before his fall, according to Hildegard, Adam was a complete and perfect musician and singer in every way. In fact, it is the devil's work to disrupt the beauty and joy of music—in fact the devil cannot sing or hold a note to speak of. The body and soul work together in music to praise God and to "radiate the Holy Spirit in the church" just as the Holy Spirit radiated Christ in the womb of Mary.[9]

Furthermore, we humans are to become musical instruments which the Holy Spirit plays. The Holy Spirit "kindles the hearts of humankind. Like tympanum and lyre it plays them, gathering volume in the temple of the soul."[10] Hildegard acknowledges feeling that she was such an instrument herself. "The marvels of God are not brought forth from one's self. Rather, it is more like a chord, a sound that is played. The tone does not come out of the chord itself, but rather, through the touch of the musician. I am, of course, the lyre and harp of God's kindness."[11] Of course, what interests Hildegard most in the present vision is that we on earth make communion with the saints by way of music. For heaven is an on-going symphony. "I saw a very bright sky in which I heard . . . in a wonderful way various kinds of music carrying on in praises of the cities of celestial joys."[12] The entire company is singing and they are singing to and about the beauty of each of the individual groups.

There are seven groups pictured in the seven rings of this illumination. In the top ring is Mary, Queen of Heaven, royal person par excellence, with the starry cosmos in the background. In this vision it is not a single voice that speaks to Hildegard but the entire communion of saints. "A sound resembling the voice of a multitude making harmony in praises from the celestial orders was uttering a symphony of Holy Mary. 'O most brilliant gem and bright glory of the sun . . . you are that translucent matter through which the very Word of God breathed out all virtues when all beings were created from their first material.' "

The next circle, reading from the top down, represents the nine orders of angels. They receive their serenade as well and are praised for being "most glorious lights," protectors of the people, who "see the inner strength of the Father." These poems to each of the circles of God's creation seem highly reminiscent of Francis of Assisi's *Canticle to Creatures* written about seventy-five years later. "Praise be to you," Hildegard sings to the angels.

The third group sung to and about are the patriarchs and prophets who are praised for "sprouting forth in the green twig." "You go around like wheels, speaking wondrously the mystical things of the mountain." They are "happy roots" who have done miracles instead of crimes in their lifetimes. The next ring depicts the apostles who have washed the devil's captives "in the fountain of living water." The martyrs are praised next who have been blessed "with the greatest joys" in the outpouring of their blood and who "rise in waves in the wounds of their own blood" to be instruments of the people of God. The sixth ring represents the confessors, those who testified to their faith short of martyrdom, as well as those who receive penitents. Hildegard praises them for always "being present to people with your help and healing powers." Next, the virgins are lauded for being a "noble greening

power rooted in the sun. You are surrounded with the embraces of divine mysteries."

Finally, Hildegard breaks into poetry and eventually song in an "Exhortation of the Virtues." The virtues are praised for being "helpers of humans" and strong "soldiers on behalf of the king of kings." Her theology of the virtues, as we saw in Vision Twenty-One above, does not moralize but celebrates virtues as personifications of powers, images of empowerment. She ends her book *Scivias* with her musical morality play—might one say opera?—called *Ordo Virtuum*, "The Play about the Virtues." In it, virtues are depicted as supporting the human soul in its difficult struggles to choose wisdom and right living. Virtues are praised for binding the devil and making a prisoner of him. And for leading the soul to the celestial city of Jerusalem. The virtues praise the human soul which has been made "on the profound height of the wisdom of God." They accompany the soul during difficult times and commiserate with the soul's suffering while they urge strength. "O fleeing soul, be strong. Clothe yourself in the armour of light." They celebrate the soul's noble decision-making with a promise that "all the heavenly army rejoices for you." That is the reason why the virtues sing their musical performance—to lead the soul to its finest destiny and rejoice with its best choices.

Hildegard chooses to end her book *Scivias* and her meditations on this vision of the communion of saints making music for the cosmos, with Psalm 150. "Praise him with the sound of trumpet; praise him with lyre and harp. Praise him with timbrel and dance. Praise him with strings and organ. Praise him with cymbals sounding forth well. Praise him with cymbals of jubilation. Let every spirit praise the Lord." Hildegard exegetes this psalm, endorsing each of the expressions of music that it invokes—including that of the "dance of exultation." For "after the timbrel, the dance exults," she tells us. "Let every spirit who has good will for believing in God and honoring him praise the Lord who is the Lord of all things. For the just one is he or she who yearns for life and God in all these amazing things God has made."[13]

One suspects that Hildegard is singing somewhere still. And is eager to make music with her sisters and brothers on earth.

A Bibliographical Note for English-Speaking Readers

The only book of Hildegard's writings in English in addition to the present one is Gabrielle Uhlein's *Meditations with Hildegard of Bingen.* (Santa Fe: 1982) Both are from Bear and Company Publishers which also plan to publish a critical English edition of *Scivias* by Dr. Bruce W. Hozeski in Fall, 1985. Bear & Co. is also planning a series of Hildegard *Readers* containing major portions of *De Operatione Dei,* of her *Letters* and of *Liber Vitae Meritorum* in 1986. A book that has been out of print for years but does contain English selections from *Scivias* in addition to a biography of Hildegard is Francesca Maria Steele, *The Life and Visions of St. Hildegard* (St. Louis: B. Herder, 1915). It is available in some libraries.

Regarding articles in English, I have found the following useful or interesting, though from a theological point of view most ought to be taken with a grain of salt until creation-centered theology penetrates more of our mystical scholarship. Peter Dronke, "The Composition of Hildegard of Bingen's *Symphonia,"* *Sacris Erudiri,* 1969-1970, pp. 381-393; Matthew Fox, "Creation-Centered Spirituality from Hildegard of Bingen to Julian of Norwich: 300 Years of an Ecological Spirituality in the West," in Philip N. Joranson and Ken Butigan, ed., *Cry of the Environment* (Santa Fe: 1984), pp. 85-106. Barbara L. Grant, "Five Liturgical Songs by Hildegard von Bingen (1098-1179)," *Signs,* Spring, 1980, pp. 557-567; Bruce W. Hozeski, "Hildegard of Bingen's 'Ordo Virtutum': The Earliest Discovered Liturgical Morality Play," *American Benedictine Review,* Summer, 1975, pp. 251-259; Bruce Hozeski, " 'Ordo Virtutum': Hildegard of Bingen's Liturgical Morality Play," Diss. (Michigan State University: 1969); Barbara J. Jeskalian, "Hildegard of Bingen, her Times and her Music," *Anima,* Fall, 1983, pp. 7-13; Sr. Ethelburg Leuschen, "Hildegarde, Saint and Scientist," *Benedictine Review,* Summer, 1958, pp. 48-53; Walter Pagel, "Hildegard of Bingen," in *Dictionary of Scientific Biography,* vol. VI (New York: 1972), pp. 396-398; George Sarton, *Introduction to the History of Science,* Vol. II (Baltimore: 1950), pp. 386-388; Bernhard W. Scholz, "Hildegard von Bingen on the Nature of Woman," *The American Benedictine Review,* December, 1980, pp. 361-383; Charles Singer, *From Magic to Science* (London: 1928), pp. 199-239; Sr. Rogatia Sohler, "Hildegard von Bingen," *Sisters Today,* January, 1980, pp. 291-296; Tom Stratman, trans., "Ordo Virtutum: The Ritual of the Virtues, by Hildegard of Bingen," (Seattle: 1984).

Acknowledgements

In addition to the persons to whom this book is dedicated I wish to thank Hildegard's Benedictine sisters who so lovingly preserved Hildegard's work over the violent centuries; Barbara and Gerry Clow for their publishing leadership and vision; Joan Ohanneson for her special Hildegardian gift; Dr. Bruce Hozeski for his persistence in getting Hildegard to English-speaking readers; Ron Miller, Robert Cunningham, Jerry Dybdal for their fine translating; Tristan for his companionship during my writing; Brendan Doyle for his steady encouragement; Marie Curran for her rapid typing; ICCS students for their assistance, questions, and eagerness to learn and live out creation mystics like Hildegard; Brian Swimme for his enthusiasm; Archbishop Hunthausen for his hospitality; Diane Schenker, James Savage and James L. Hermann for their memorable rendition of "Ordo Virtutum" in Seattle's Cathedral; and to Barbara Clow for her index of the text.

References for Parts I & II

1. Barbara Thornton, "The Musical Conception of Ordo Virtutum." These notes accompany the record, *Hildegard von Bingen: Ordo Virtutum, Sequentia Ensemble für Musik des Mittelalters,* WDR Producer, EMI Electrola, Cologne, Germany, 1982.

2. The poems are contained in Pudentiana Barth, et. al., *Hildegard von Bingen: Lieder* (Salzburg: 1969), hereafter referred to as *Lieder. Hildegardis Scivias,* ed. Adelgundis Fuhrkotter, *Corpus Christianorum Continuatio Mediaevalis,* 43, 43A (Turnhaut 1978). Hereafter, *Scivias.* Heinrich Schipperges, trans. *Hildegard von Bingen, Welt und Mensch* (Salzburg: 1965). This critical German translation of Hildegard's *De Operatione Dei* will henceforth be abbreviated, *DOD;* Adelgundis Fuhrkotter, transl., *Hildegard von Bingen, Brief-wechsel* (Salzburg: 1965). This German translation of Hildegard's Letters will henceforth be abbreviated, *Brief.*

3. *Brief.*, p. 111. Translations of these letters by Ron Miller.

4. Wolfgang Seibrich, "Zur Geschichte des Disibodenberges," in H.A. Ederer, ed., *Der Disibodenberg* (Sobernheim: n.d.), p. 12.

5. Joannes Paulus PP.II, "Pope's Letter to Cardinal Volk, Bishop of Mainz," *L'Osservatore Romano* (October 1, 1979), p. 10.

6. *Scivias,* pp. 3f.,5. Translations are mine.

7. *Ibid.*, pp. 400, 536.

8. Gabrriele Uhlein, *Meditations with Hildegard of Bingen* (Santa Fe: 1982), pp. 40, 37. Hereafter, abbreviated Uhlein.

9. *Scivias,* p. 4.

10. *Ibid.*, p. 8.

11. *Ibid.*, p. 635.

12. *DOD.*, p. 58. Translations by Robert Cunningham.

13. Wendell C. Beane, William G. Doty, eds., *Myths, Rites, Symbols: A Mircea Eliade Reader,* vol. II, (New York: 1976), pp. 338f. Henceforth, Eliade.

14. *Scivias,* p. xxxiv.

15. See J. Schomer, *Die Illustrationen der hl. Hildegard von Bingen* als *kunstlerische Neuschopfung* (Diss.), Bonn: 1937; Ch. Meier, *Text und Bild im uberlieferten Werk Hildegarde von Bingen* (Wiesbaden, 1978).

16. Marianna Schrader, Adelgundis Fuhrkotter, *Die Echtheit der Schrifttums der heiligen Hildegard von Bingen* (Cologne: 1956).

17. *DOD,* p. 10.

18. *Ibid.*, p. 318.

19. *Scivias,* p. 554.

20. *Brief.*, p. 124. For another analysis of Hildegard's creation theology and its gift to our times in light of other Rhineland mystics, see Matthew Fox, "Creation-Centered Spirituality from Hildegard of Bingen to Julian of Norwich: 300 Years of an Ecological Spirituality in the West," in Philip N. Joranson and Ken Butigan, ed., *Cry of the Environment* (Santa Fe: 1984), pp. 85-106.

21. See Matthew Fox, *Original Blessing: A Primer in Creation Spirituality* (Santa Fe: 1984). Henceforth, *Original Blessing.*

22. *DOD,* p. 252.

23. *Scivias,* p. 59.

24. *Brief.*, p. 105.

25. *Ibid.*, p. 25.

26. Sue Woodruff, *Meditations with Mechtild of Magdeburg* (Santa Fe: 1983), p. 18.

27. Bernhard W. Scholz, "Hildegard von Bingen on the Nature of Woman," *The American Benedictine Review* (December, 1980), p. 361. See also, pp. 375ff.

28. Uhlein, p. 101.

29. Scholz, *art. cit.*, pp. 379f.

30. *Brief,* p. 26.

31. Scholz, *art. cit.*, pp. 370f.

32. Uhlein, p. 124.

33. *Ibid.*, p. 105.

34. *Ibid.*, p. 65.

35. M.D. Chenu, "Body and Body Politic in the Creation Spirituality of Thomas Aquinas," in Matthew Fox, ed., *Western Spirituality: Historical Roots, Ecumenical Routes* (Santa Fe: 1981), p. 212.

36. *Ibid.*, p. 214, note 20. See Thomas Aquinas, *De Potentia,* 3, 16; *Sum. theol.*, q. 47, a.3.

37. Matthew Fox, *Breakthrough: Meister Eckhart's Creation Spirituality in New Translation* (Garden City, 1980), pp. 30-35. Henceforth, *Breakthrough:*.

38. Giuseppe Tucci, *The Theory and Practice of the Mandala* (London: 1961), p. 86.

39. *Ibid.*, p. 54.

40. Uhlein, pp. 110, 71.

41. C. G. Jung, *The Secret of the Golden Flower* (New York, 1962), p. 144.

42. Cited in Tucci, *op. cit.*, pp. 28f.

43. *Ibid.*, p. 29.

44. Uhlein, p. 127.

45. *Ibid.*, p. 126.

46. Laurens van der Post, "Wilderness: A Way of Truth," *One Earth* (Summer/October, 1984), pp. 6, 4.

47. M.D. Chenu, *Nature, Man and Society in the Twelfth Century* (Chicago: 1968), p. 5.

48. *Ibid.*, pp. 6f.

49. *Ibid.*, p. 35.

50. Uhlein, p. 49.

51. Chenu, *op. cit.*, p. 35.

52. Uhlein, p. 78-80.

53. S.G.F. Brandon, *Man and God in Art and Ritual* (New York: 1975), p. 385.

54. *Ibid.*, p. 3.

55. Eliade, p. 345.

56. *Ibid.*, p. 351.

57. Chenu, *op. cit.*, pp. 99, 101.

58. See Matthew Fox, *Whee! We, wee All the Way Home: A Guide to a Sensual, Prophetic Spirituality* (Santa Fe: 1981).

References for Part III

Illumination One: The Man in Sapphire Blue: A Study in Compassion

1. *Scivias*, p. 124. This illumination is the Second Vision of the Second Part of *Scivias*, pp. 124-132.

2. *Brief.*, pp. 68, 70.

3. Eliade, p. 416.

4. *Brief.*, p 67.

5. Uhlein, p. 21.

6. *Ibid.*, p. 90.

7. *Ibid.*, p. 36.

8. *Brief.*, p. 74.

9. *Ibid.*, p. 84.

10. See *Breakthrough*, Sermons 30, 31.

11. *Scivias*, p. 435.

12. Uhlein, p. 91.

13. *Scivias*, p. 127. Cf. Matthew Fox, *A Spirituality Named Compassion* (Minneapolis: 1979).

14. Tucci, *op. cit.*, p. 25.

15. *Scivias*, p. 84.

16. Tucci, p. 26.

17. *Breakthrough*, p. 441.

Illumination Two: Hildegard's Awakening: A Self-Portrait

1. *Scivias*, pp. 5f. This illumination is the "Protestificatio" and introduction to *Scivias*, pp. 3-6.

2. *Ibid.*, p. 3.

3. *DOD*, p. 171.

4. *Brief*, p. 109.

5. *Ibid.*, p. 82.

6. "De Spiritu Sancto," in *Lieder*, p. 228. Translation by Fr. Jerry Dybdal.

7. Patricia Janis Broder, *Hopi Painting: The World of the Hopis* (New York: 1978), p. 92.

8. David Maclagan, *Creation Myths* (New York: 1977), p. 26.

9. Eliade, pp. 365f.

10. Cf. Barry Fell, *America B.C.* (New York: 1978).

Illumination Three: Viriditas: Greening Power

1. Uhlein, p. 49; *Brief.*, p. 136.

2. *Lieder*, p. 314. Translation by Tom Stratman.

3. J. P. Migne, *Patrologia latina*, vol. 197 (Paris: 1885), 377C; 818d/d. Hereafter, *PL*.

4. Uhlein, pp. 115, 119.

5. *Breakthrough*, p. 251. See also Sermons 20-29, the Via Creativa in Eckhart's theology.

6. *Lieder*, p. 244. Translation by Fr. Jerry Dybdal.

7. Uhlein, p. 88.

8. *Ibid.*, p. 54.

9. *Ibid.*, p. 31.

Illumination Four: Egg of the Universe

1. *Scivias*, p. 42. This illumination is the Third Vision of the First Part of *Scivias*, pp. 40-59.

2. J.E. Cirlot, *A Dictionary of Symbols* (New York: 1962), p. 90. Hereafter, Cirlot.

3. Charles Singer, *From Magic to Science* (London: 1928), p. 207.

4. Cited in Sr. Ethelburg Leuschen, "Hildegarde, Saint and Scientist," *Benedictine Review* (Summer, 1958), p. 52.

5. Otto Rank, *Beyond Psychology* (New York: 1941).

6. Uhlein, p. 65.

7. *Ibid.*, . 41.

8. *Breakthrough*, p. 198.

9. Uhlein, p. 106.

10. *Ibid.*, p. 125.

11. *Ibid.*, p. 107.

12. *Scivias*, p. 40.

13. *Ibid.*, Subsequent citations in this section are from *Scivias*, pp. 40f. unless otherwise noted.

14. *Ibid.*, p. 51.

15. *Ibid.*, p. 57.

16. Cf. Psalms 89, 82. See *Original Blessing,* pp. 66-88.

17. *Scivias*, pp. 57f.

18. *Ibid.*, p. 43. Subsequent citations are from *Scivias,* pp. 43-47.

Illumination Five: The Cosmic Wheel

1. *DOD*, p. 35. This illumination is the second vision in *DOD*, pp. 35-60, entitled "On the Construction of the World."

2. Cirlot, p. 67.

3. *DOD*, p. 25.

4. *Ibid.*, p. 27.

5. *Ibid.*, p. 25.

6. *Ibid.*, p. 35. Subsequent citations are taken from this section, pp. 35-37.

7. *Ibid.*, pp. 44f.

8. *Ibid.*, p. 52.

9. *Ibid.*, p. 59.

10. Uhlein, p. 36.

11. *Ibid.*, p. 90.

Illumination Six: The Human as Microcosm of the Macrocosm

1. *DOD*, p. 61. This illumination is the third vision in *DOD*, entitled "On Human Nature," pp. 61-78. Subsequent citations are from pp. 61f. unless otherwise stated.

2. Uhlein, p. 105.

3. In *DOD,* p. 15.

4. *Ibid.*, pp. 16f.

5. *DOD*, p. 62.

6. *Ibid.*, p. 66.

7. *Ibid.*, p. 67.

8. *Ibid.*, p. 68.

9. See *Original Blessing,* Themes 4 and 22-26.

10. *DOD*, p. 74.

11. *Ibid.*, p. 70.

12. *Ibid.*, p. 73.

13. *Ibid.*, p. 74.

14. *Ibid.*, p. 75.

15. *Ibid.*, p. 65.

16. *Ibid.*, pp. 77f.

Illumination Seven: Cultivating the Cosmic Tree

1. Cirlot, p. 328.

2. *DOD*, p. 83. This illumination is the fourth vision in *DOD*, entitled "On the Articulation of the Body," pp. 79-184.

3. *Ibid.*, pp. 83f.

4. Eliade, pp. 328f.

5. *DOD*, pp. 79, 81. Subsequent citations in this section are from pp. 87-104 unless otherwise stated.

6. *Ibid.*, p. 87.

7. *Ibid.*, p. 106

8. Cirlot, p. 331.

9. *DOD*, p. 100

10. *Ibid.*, p. 107

11. *Ibid.*, p. 170.

12. *Ibid.*, p. 165.

13. *Ibid.*, p. 171.

Illumination Eight: The Creator's Glory, Creation's Glory

1. *Scivias*, pp. 327ff. This illumination is the First Vision of the Third Part of *Scivias,* pp. 327-347.

2. Cirlot, p. 3.

3. *Scivias*, p. 332.

4. See Helen Kenik, "Toward a Biblical Basis for Creation Theology," in Matthew Fox, ed., *Western Spirituality, op. cit.,* pp. 32-61; and *Original Blessing* , pp. 93-102.

5. *Scivias*, p. 329. Subsequent citations in this section are from pp. 330-332 unless otherwise noted.

6. Cirlot, p. 323.

7. *Brief.*, p. 136.

8. *Ibid.*, p. 126.

9. *Ibid.*, pp. 140f.

10. *Ibid.*, p. 70.

11. *Scivias*, pp. 340f.

Illumination Nine: Original Blessing: The Golden Tent

1. *Scivias*, p. 91. This illumination is the Fourth Vision of the First Part of *Scivias,* pp. 60-92.

2. C. G. Jung in *The Collected Works of C.G. Jung,* vol. X (Princeton: 1970), 403-406.

3. *Scivias*, p. 61.

4. *Ibid.*, p. 72.

5. *Ibid.*, p. 78.

6. See Brian Swimme, *The Universe is a Green Dragon* (Santa Fe: 1984), pp. 127-139, 27.

7. *Scivias*, p. 78.

8. *Ibid.*, p. 62. Subsequent citations in this section are from pp. 62-68 unless otherwise noted.

9. *Ibid.*, p. 70.

10. *Ibid.*, p. 75.

11. *Ibid.*, p. 87. Subsequent citations in this section are from pp. 88-92.

Illumination Ten: Adam's Fall

1. *Scivias*, p. 14. This illumination is the Second Vision of the First Part of *Scivias*, pp. 12-38. Subsequent citations in this section are from pp. 12-14 unless otherwise noted.

2. *Ibid.*, p. 32.

3. *Ibid.*, p. 19.

4. *Ibid.*, p. 20.

5. *Ibid.*, p. 36.

6. Cirlot, p. 239.

7. *Scivias*, p. 36.

8. *Scivias*, p. 334.

9. *Brief.*, p. 112.

Illumination Eleven: Recycling Lucifer's Fall into Humanity's Glory

1. *Scivias*, p. 341. This illumination is a second one within the First Vision of the Third Part of *Scivias*, pp. 341-347. Subsequent citations in this section are from pp. 341-343.

2. *Ibid.*, p. 345.

3. *Breakthrough*, pp. 107-110.

4. Uhlein, p. 53.

5. *Scivias*, p. 347.

Illumination Twelve: Sin—Drying Up

1. *Scivias*, pp. 465, 462. This illumination is the Seventh Vision of the Third Part of *Scivias*, pp. 462-476.

2. *Ibid.*, p. 471.

3. *Ibid.*, p. 473.

4. Cirlot, pp. 308f.

5. *DOD*, p. 47.

6. *Ibid.*, p. 98.

7. *Ibid.*, p. 75.

8. Uhlein, p. 76.

9. *Scivias*, p. 55.

10. *Ibid.*, pp. 14, 16.

11. *DOD*, p. 74.

12. Uhlein, p. 120.

13. *DOD*, p. 70.

14. *PL* 764; 194.

15. *Scivias*, p. 470.

16. *DOD*, p. 58.

17. *Scivias*, p. 468. Subsequent citations in this section are from *Scivias*, pp. 468-470.

18. Uhlein, p. 109.

19. *Ibid.*, p. 63.

Illumination Thirteen: The Six Days of Creation Renewed

1. *Scivias*, p. 112. This illumination is the First Vision of the Second Part of *Scivias*, pp. 109-123.

2. *DOD*, p. 26.

3. *Scivias*, p. 115.

4. Cirlot, p. 95.

5. *Brief.*, p. 68.

6. *Scivias*, p. 115.

7. *Ibid.*, p. 338.

8. *Ibid.*, p. 115.

9. *Ibid.*, p. 116.

10. *Ibid.*, p. 113.

11. *Ibid.*, p. 117.

12. *Ibid.*, pp. 111, 121.

13. *Ibid.*, p. 114. Subsequent citations in this section are from pp. 114-122.

14. Cf. *Breakthrough*, pp. 154, 267-72.

Illumination Fourteen: Sophia: Mother Wisdom, Mother Church

1. Evola, cited in Cirlot, p. 208.

2. *Ibid.*, p. 217.

3. *Scivias*, p. 305.

4. Cirlot, p. 267.

5. *Ibid.*, p. 103.

6. *Scivias*, p. 175. Subsequent citations in this section are from *Scivias*, pp. 175-177. This illumination is the Fifth Vision of the Second Part of *Scivias*, pp. 172-224. Subsequent citations in this section are from pp. 175-177.

7. *Ibid.*, p. 204.

8. *Ibid.*, pp. 199f.

9. Chenu, *Nature, Man and Society in the Twelfth Century*, *op. cit.*, pp. 208-211.

10. *Scivias*, p. 190.

11. *Ibid.*, p. 178.

12. See Rosemary Ruether, "Patristic Spirituality and the Experience of Women in the Early Church," in Matthew Fox, ed., *Western Spirituality*, *op. cit.*, pp. 151f.

13. See Matthew Fox, *Breakthrough*, Sermon 20.

14. *Scivias*, p. 195. Subsequent citations in this section are from pp. 195-197.

15. Sr. Magna Ungrund, *Die Metaphysisch Anthropologie der H1. Hildegard von Bingin*, (Munster: 1938), p. 88. For more on Hildegard's views on sexuality, see Scholtz, *art. cit.*

16. *Scivias*, p. 208.

17. *Ibid.*, p. 221.

18. *Ibid.*, p. 187.

19. *Ibid.*, p. 204.

20. See *Breakthrough*, p. 110-113.

21. *Scivias*, p. 135.

Illumination Fifteen: All Beings Celebrate Creation

1. *Scivias*, p. 100. This illumination is the Sixth Vision of the First Part of *Scivias*, pp. 100-108. Subsequent citations in this section are from pp. 100-103.

2. Cirlot, pp. 69f.

3. See Matthew Fox, *A Spirituality Named Compassion, op. cit.*, Chapter Two, "From Climbing Jacob's Ladder to Dancing Sarah's Circle," pp. 36-67.

4. *Scivias*, p. 107.

5. Uhlein, p. 65.

6. *Ibid.*, p. 41.

7. Cirlot, p. 73.

8. *Ibid.*, p. 223.

9. David Maclagan, *Creation Myths, op. cit.*, pp. 60f.

Illumination Sixteen: Emptying The True Spirit of Poverty

1. *Scivias*, p. 7. This illumination is the First Vision of the First Part of *Scivias*, pp. 7-11. Subsequent citations in this section are from pp. 7-11 unless otherwise noted.

2. Cirlot, p. 95.

3. *Ibid.*

4. *Brief.*, p. 68.

5. C.G. Jung, *Symbols of Transformation* (Princeton:1956), p. 268.

6. Cirlot, p. 95.

7. See *Breakthrough*, Sermon Fifteen.

8. See *ibid.*, pp. 129-150.

9. Eliade, pp. 379f.

10. Cirlot, p. 209.

11. Eliade, p. 374.

12. *Lieder*, p. 244.

13. *Scivias*, p. 8.

Illumination Seventeen: Strengthening the Soul for the Journey

1. *Scivias*, p. 88. This illumination is the second one within the Fourth Vision of the First Part of *Scivias*, pp. 60-92. Subsequent citations in this section are from pp. 88-92 unless otherwise noted.

2. Cirlot, p. 58.

3. *Ibid.*, p. 57.

4. *Ibid.*, p. 241.

5. *Scivias*, p. 83. Subsequent citations in this section are from pp. 83-91 unless otherwise noted.

6. Cirlot, pp. 244; 58.

7. *Scivias*, p. 83.

8. *Ibid.*, p. 87.

9. *Ibid.*, p. 91.

10. *Breakthrough*, p. 441.

11. *Scivias*, p. 87.

12. *Lieder*, pp. 270, 272.

13. *Scivias*, p. 92.

Illumination Eighteen: Powers, Principalities and Antichrist

1. *Scivias*, p. 576. This illumination is the Eleventh Visiion of the Third Part of *Scivias*, pp. 574-603. Subsequent citations in this section are from pp. 576-583.

2. Cirlot, p. 299.

3. *Scivias*, pp. 586f. Subsequent citations in this section are from pp. 586-594.

4. See *Original Blessing*, pp. 70-80.

5. *Scivias*, pp. 596f.

6. *Ibid.*, pp. 600, 603.

Illumination Nineteen: The Crucifixion and The Mass: Cosmic Events

1. *Scivias*, p. 232. This illumination is the Sixth Vision of the Second Part of *Scivias*, pp. 225-306. Subsequent

citations in this section are from pp. 230-233 unless otherwise stated.

2. *Ibid.*, p. 245.

3. *Ibid.*, p. 35.

4. *Ibid.*, pp. 235, 236.

5. Cirlot, pp. 115f.

6. *Scivias*, p. 234. Subsequent citations in this section are from pp. 230-234 unless otherwise noted.

7. *Ibid.*, p. 266.

8. *Ibid.*, pp. 250f. Subsequent citations in this section are from pp. 251-261.

9. See Meister Eckhart's sermon: "Compassion as Celebration," in *Breakthrough*, pp. 531-545.

10. *Scivias*, p. 298.

11. *Ibid.*, p. 299.

12. Uhlein, p. 128.

Illumination Twenty: The Mystical Body Taming the Devil

1. *Scivias*, pp. 308f. This illumination is the Seventh Vision of the Second Part of *Scivias*, pp. 307-325. Subsequent citations in this section are from pp. 317-323 unless otherwise noted.

2. Cirlot, p. 13.

3. *Ibid.*, p. 19.

4. *Scivias*, p. 308. Subsequent citations in this section are from pp. 308-311 unless otherwise noted.

5. Uhlein, p. 90.

6. *Scivias*, p. 324.

7. *Ibid.*, p. 323.

8. *Ibid.*, p. 324.

9. *Ibid.*, pp. 312, 324.

10. *Ibid.*, p. 312.

11. See *Breakthrough*. Sermon 30. Also, Matthew Fox, "Meister Eckhart and Karl Marx: The Mystic as Political Theologian,' in Richard Woods, ed., *Understanding Mysticism* (Garden City: 1980), pp. 541-563.

12. *Scivias*, p. 313.

Illumination Twenty-One: Five Virtues Building a Heavenly City in the House of Wisdom

1. *Scivias*, p. 547. This illumination is the Tenth Vision of the Third Part of *Scivias*, pp. 545-573.

2. *Ibid.*, p. 551. Subsequent citations in this section are from pp. 549-551 unless otherwise noted.

3. *Ibid.*, p. 557.

4. *Ibid.*, pp. 551, 554.

5. *Ibid.*, p. 549.

6. Cirlot, p. 146.

7. *Scivias*, pp. 570, 573.

8. *Ibid*, pp. 566, 559.

9. Cirlot, p. 294.

10. *Breakthrough*, p. 440.

11. *Scivias*, p. 559.

12. *Ibid.*, pp. 568f.

13. *Ibid.*, p. 560. Subsequent citations in this section are from pp. 560-566.

Illumination Twenty-Two: The Red Head of God Zealous for Erotic Justice

1. *Scivias*, p. 430. This illumination is the Fifth Vision of the Third Part of *Scivias*, pp. 408-431.

2. *Ibid.*, p. 429.

3. *Ibid.*, p. 363.

4. *Ibid.*, p. 366.

5. *Ibid.*, p. 352.

6. C.G. Jung, *Symbols of Transformation, op. cit.*, p. 208.

7. *Scivias*, p. 356. Subsequent citations in this section are from pp. 353-356 unless otherwise noted.

8. Cirlot, p. 47.

9. *Scivias*, p. 356.

10. *Lieder*, p. 312.

11. *DOD*, p. 169.

12. *Scivias*, p. 360.

13. *Ibid.*, p. 423.

14. *Ibid.*, p. 411. Subsequent citations in this section are from pp. 411-428 unless otherwise noted.

15. Cited in Ungrund, *op. cit.*, p. 67.

16. *Scivias*, pp. 413, 415.

17. *Ibid.*, p. 424.

18. For more on "erotic justice," *Original Blessing*, pp. 177-306.

19. *Lieder*, pp. 276, 278. Translation by Fr. Jerry Dybdal.

20. Cirlot, pp. 354f.

21. *Uhlein*, p. 85.

22. Many commentators on western mysticism of the past few centuries have completely distorted the meaning of "speculative mysticism," implying that spirituality for certain mystics was a matter of idle theologizing. Hildegard would recommend that such people quit projecting Cartesian dualistic knowledge theories onto

the mystics of the past and spend more time with the mirrors of God and mirrors of Christ in themselves and in all creatures.

23. *Lieder,* p. 282.

Illumination Twenty-Three: Redemption: Cosmic Healing, Cosmic Regeneration

1. *Scivias,* p. 604. This illumination is the Twelfth Vision of the Third Part of *Scivias,* pp. 604-613. Subsequent citations in this section are from pp. 604-608.

2. *Ibid.,* p. 611. Subsequent citations in this section are from pp. 607-613.

3. *Ibid.,* p. 606.

4. Eliade, pp. 433f.

5. Cirlot, p. 158.

6. *Scivias,* p. 607.

7. Cirlot, pp. 50-53.

8. *Scivias,* p. 613.

Illumination Twenty-Four: New Heaven, New Earth

1. *DOD,* p. 60.

2. *Scivias,* p. 605. This illumination is a second one within the Twelfth Vision of the Third Part of *Scivias,* pp. 604-613. Subsequent citations in this section are from pp. 604-609 unless otherwise noted.

3. Cirlot, p. 73.

4. See Sermon 27, "How All Creatures Experience the Divine Repose," in *Breakthrough,* pp. 380-387.

5. *Scivias,* pp. 612, 610.

6. Cirlot, p. 103.

7. *Uhlein,* p. 89.

8. *Ibid.,* p. 87.

Illumination Twenty-Five: The Communion of Saints in Cosmic Symphony

1. Uhlein, p. 111.

2. *Ibid.,* p. 127.

3. *Ibid.,* p. 128.

4. *DOD,* p. 170.

5. *Ibid.*

6. Uhlein, p. 28.

7. *Scivias,* p. 630. This illumination is the Thirteenth Vision of the Third Part of *Scivias,* pp. 614-636. It is the last vision of *Scivias* as it is in the present book. Subsequent citations in this section are from pp. 630-632 unless otherwise noted.

8. J.B. Pitra, *Analecta sacra,* vol. VIII, (Monte Cassino: 1882), p. 352.

9. *Brief.,* pp. 239f. A portion of this letter is translated into English in Carol Neuls-Bates, ed., *Women in Music* (New York: 1982), pp. 14-20.

10. Uhlein, p. 37.

11. *Ibid.,* p. 93.

12. *Scivias,* p. 614. Subsequent citations in this section are from pp. 614-616 unless otherwise noted.

13. *Ibid.,* pp. 634-636. Cf. Meister Eckhart's final sermon in *Breakthrough,* "Compassion as Celebration," pp. 531-545.

INDEX